Contributing Editors
Heather Douglas
Lorin Klistoff, M.A.

Managing Editor
Karen J. Goldfluss, M.S. Ed.

Cover Artist
Brenda DiAntonis

Art Production Manager
Kevin Barnes

Art Coordinator
Renée Christine Yates

Imaging
James Edward Grace
Ricardo Martinez

Publisher
Mary D. Smith, M.S. Ed.

DAILY WARM
Reading
GRADE 3

- Over 150 nonfiction and fiction passages
- Follow-up questions for each passage target essential comprehension skills.
- Ideal for test preparation!

D1399299

Author

Shelle Russell

Teacher
Created
Resources

Teacher Created Resources, Inc.
6421 Industry Way
Westminster, CA 92683
www.teachercreated.com

ISBN: 978-1-4206-3489-1

©2006 Teacher Created Resources, Inc.
Reprinted, 2011
Made in U.S.A.

Table of Contents

Introduction 4

Tracking Sheet 6

Nonfiction 7

Animals 9

Squirrels—Sparrows—Hummingbirds—Cat Myths—Rats—Ants—Crows—
Horses—Interesting Bird—Ducks—Raccoons—Milking Cows—Pigs—
Herding Dogs—Sheep—Goats—Geese—Chickens

Biography 27

Daniel Boone—Johnny Appleseed—Sacagawea—Davy Crockett—Narcissa
Whitman—Stagecoach Mary Fields—Clara Barton—Charlie Parkhurst—
Dr. Antonia Novello—Louis Pasteur—Elizabeth Blackwell—Cesar Chavez—
Calamity Jane—Sally Ride—Annie Oakley—Dale Evans—Patrick Henry—
Betsy Ross

American History 45

Ghost Town—Pony Express—Railroads—Trading Posts on the Oregon
Trail—Colonial Tools and Weapons—Colonial Animals—The Wilderness—
Colonial Gardens—Diaries—Racing to the Gold—Gold Country '49—Civil
War Weapons—Map Skills—Declaration of Independence—Jamestown—
Colonial Williamsburg—Communities Long Ago—Communities Today

Science 63

Classifying Animals—Plants—Forests—Oceans—Deserts—Tundra—
Tropical Rainforests—Brain Power—Soft T-Rex—New Planet?

Current Events 73

Recycling—Citizen Test—What Is a Blog?—Cosmic DNA Surprise—
Commanding Officer—Turnoff Weeks—What the President Can't Do—
Saving the Movies—Hospital Technology—Habitat for Humanity—AYSO
Soccer—Opportunities for Kids—Kids' Clubs—Jury Duty

Table of Contents

Fiction 87

   Fairy Tales and Folklore 89

   Marsha—Three Little Ants—Jessie and the Cornstalk—Little Brown
   Hummingbird—Three Sister Sheep— Penny Loafer and the Three Monkeys—
   Peter and Patty—Sky Blue—Lizard Prince—The Sloth and the Tiger—Goofy
   Goose—Little Banana Girl—Why Ants Bite Legs at Picnics—Beetle Boy and
   the Talking Coconut—Speeding Spider—Prince and the Pebble

   Historical Fiction 105

   The Time Machine—Kwakiutl—Cheyenne—Navajo Landing—
   Wampanoag—Mayflower Adventure—Patrick Henry's Influence—George
   Washington's Letter—Thomas Jefferson's Day Off—Paul Revere's Stories—
   Martha Washington's Party—Florence Nightingale's Visit—Mother Teresa's
   Ride—Rosa Parks's Tale—Princess Diana Shares—Dolley Madison

   Contemporary Realistic Fiction 121

   Math Mania—Write On—Shoot the Hoops—All-Star Soccer—Baseball
   Days—Harvest Festival—Beach Days—Skiing in the Mountains—A Day
   in the Park—San Francisco—Faces in South Dakota—Bad Hair Day—No
   Homework—Best Friends—Exchange Student—Moving Day—Ski Pants

   Mystery/Suspense/Adventure 138

   Ray's Smirk—Missing Key—Moving Light—Abandoned Bus—Chocolate
   Snapshot—Missing Dog—Called for Cheating—A Haunted House?—Secret
   Code—Letters in the Mail—Socks—Cyclone in the House

   Fantasy 150

   Jelly Bean Planet—My Day as a Pancake—Life of a Flower—Super Girl—
   Trading Places—Talking Horse—Animal Picnic—At the Zoo—Exploring
   the Galaxy—Couch Cookie—Jellyfish Surprise—Talking Toaster—Lori
   Lollipop—Strawberry Patch—Invasion of the Animals—Vanishing Veggies—
   Egyptian Ants in the Bathroom

Answer Key 167

Leveling Chart 175

Certificate 176

Introduction

The goal of this book is to help children improve their skills in both reading and comprehension on a daily basis. The more experience a child has with reading, the stronger his or her reading and problem-solving skills will become. *Daily Warm Ups: Reading (Grade 3)* is composed of passages that provide both factual and fictional material. Questions that follow are based on Bloom's Taxonomy, higher-level thinking skills, and national standards that are required for grade three learners. Using this book in your daily routine will boost children's reading and comprehension scores significantly.

Nonfiction and Fiction

Daily Warm-Ups: Reading (Grade 3) is divided into two sections: fiction (narrative) and nonfiction (expository). Each of the two sections is divided into five categories. The nonfiction section includes the following: animals, biographies, American history, science, and current events. The fiction section includes the following: fairy tales and folklore, historical fiction, contemporary realistic fiction, mystery/adventure/suspense, and fantasy.

Because understanding both types of literature is extremely important to our students' success, exposure to both fiction and nonfiction reading is essential. Questions which follow the passages are strategically written to address concepts and strategies that are required nationwide.

Comprehension Questions

Comprehension is the most important goal of any reading assignment. Students who comprehend what they read perform better in class, score higher on tests, and perform tasks in life more confidently. Questions that follow the reading passages are written to encourage students to recognize structure of the text, visualize, summarize, learn new vocabulary, and implement strategies for breaking words into parts for better comprehension. Reading skills used in *Daily Warm-Ups: Reading (Grade 3)* can also be found in scope and sequence charts across the nation. Different types of questions are written to help students become more confident in the following:

- Comparing/contrasting
- Recognizing facts/opinions
- Synonyms
- Author purpose
- Antonyms
- Recognizing main idea
- Word structure

- Understanding vocabulary
- Recalling details
- Similes
- Making inferences
- Idioms
- Drawing conclusions
- Describing character traits

Introduction

Readability

Each of the reading passages in *Daily Warm-Ups: Reading (Grade 3)* varies in difficulty to meet the various reading levels of your students. The passages have been categorized as follows: below grade level, at grade level, and above grade level. (See Leveling Chart on page 175.)

Record Keeping

Use the tracking sheet on page 6 to record which warm-up exercises you have given to your students. Or, distribute copies of the sheet for students to keep their own records. Use the certificate on page 176 as you see fit. You can use the certificate as a reward for students completing a certain number of warm-up exercises. Or, you may choose to distribute the certificates to students who complete the warm-up exercises with 100% accuracy.

How to Make the Most of This Book

Here are some simple tips, which you may have already thought of, already implemented, or may be new to you. They are only suggestions to help you make your students as successful in reading as possible.

- Read through the book ahead of time so you are familiar with each portion. The better you understand how the book works, the easier it will be to answer students' questions.

- Set aside a regular time each day to incorporate *Daily Warm-Ups* into your routine. Once the routine is established, students will look forward to working on and expect to work on reading strategies at that particular time.

- Make sure that any amount of time spent on *Daily Warm-Ups* is positive and constructive. This should be a time of practicing for success and recognizing it as it is achieved.

- Allot only about five minutes to *Daily Warm-Ups*. Too much time will not be useful; too little time will create additional stress.

- Be sure to model the reading and question-answering process at the beginning of the year before students attempt to do the passages on their own. Modeling for about five days in a row seems to be a good start. Model pre-reading questions, reading the passage, highlighting information that refers to the questions, and eliminating answers that are obviously wrong. Finally, refer back to the text once again, to make sure the answers chosen are the best ones.

- Create and store overheads of each lesson so that you can review student work, concepts, and strategies as quickly as possible.

- Utilize peer tutors who have strong skills for peer interaction to assist struggling students.

- Offer small group time to students who need extra enrichment or opportunities for questions regarding the text. Small groups will allow many of these students, once they are comfortable with the format, to achieve success independently.

- Adjust the procedures, as you see fit, to meet the needs of all your students.

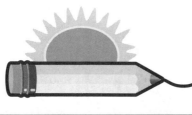

Tracking Sheet

NONFICTION

Animals		Biography		American History		Science		Current Events	
Page 9		Page 27		Page 45		Page 63		Page 73	
Page 10		Page 28		Page 46		Page 64		Page 74	
Page 11		Page 29		Page 47		Page 65		Page 75	
Page 12		Page 30		Page 48		Page 66		Page 76	
Page 13		Page 31		Page 49		Page 67		Page 77	
Page 14		Page 32		Page 50		Page 68		Page 78	
Page 15		Page 33		Page 51		Page 69		Page 79	
Page 16		Page 34		Page 52		Page 70		Page 80	
Page 17		Page 35		Page 53		Page 71		Page 81	
Page 18		Page 36		Page 54		Page 72		Page 82	
Page 19		Page 37		Page 55				Page 83	
Page 20		Page 38		Page 56				Page 84	
Page 21		Page 39		Page 57				Page 85	
Page 22		Page 40		Page 58				Page 86	
Page 23		Page 41		Page 59					
Page 24		Page 42		Page 60					
Page 25		Page 43		Page 61					
Page 26		Page 44		Page 62					

FICTION

Fairy Tales and Folklore		Historical Fiction		Contemporary Realistic Fiction		Mystery/Suspense/ Adventure		Fantasy	
Page 89		Page 105		Page 121		Page 138		Page 150	
Page 90		Page 106		Page 122		Page 139		Page 151	
Page 91		Page 107		Page 123		Page 140		Page 152	
Page 92		Page 108		Page 124		Page 141		Page 153	
Page 93		Page 109		Page 125		Page 142		Page 154	
Page 94		Page 110		Page 126		Page 143		Page 155	
Page 95		Page 111		Page 127		Page 144		Page 156	
Page 96		Page 112		Page 128		Page 145		Page 157	
Page 97		Page 113		Page 129		Page 146		Page 158	
Page 98		Page 114		Page 130		Page 147		Page 159	
Page 99		Page 115		Page 131		Page 148		Page 160	
Page 100		Page 116		Page 132		Page 149		Page 161	
Page 101		Page 117		Page 133				Page 162	
Page 102		Page 118		Page 134				Page 163	
Page 103		Page 119		Page 135				Page 164	
Page 104		Page 120		Page 136				Page 165	
				Page 137				Page 166	

NONFICTION

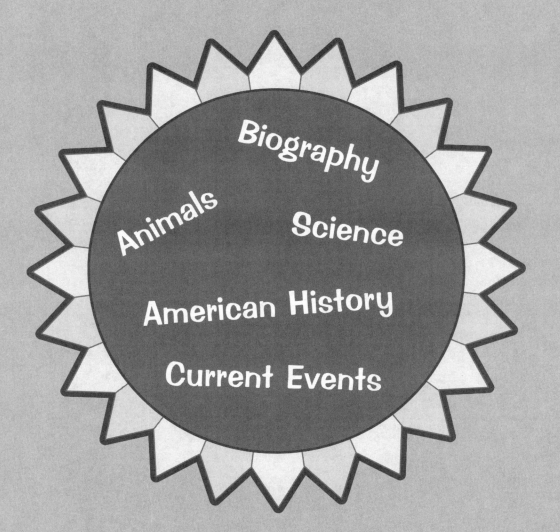

Biography

Animals

Science

American History

Current Events

Name _____   Date _____

SQUIRRELS

Squirrels are exciting. In the summer, they run around right after the sun comes up. In the afternoon, the squirrels go back to their nests. They take naps. Two hours before the sun goes down, they get up and run around again. When it is dark outside at night, they stay inside their nests.

Squirrels are busiest of all in the wintertime. They run fast. They make turns in the air. Squirrels jump from tree branch to tree branch. They run all morning until lunch. After lunch, they go back to their nests to rest again. When the weather is bad, they do not leave their nests. However, they do not hibernate, or sleep all winter.

Squirrels have eyes on the top of their heads. These eyes help them to see objects without having to turn their heads. These eyes are difficult, too. They make it hard for the squirrel when it is eating. The squirrel's eyes are busy watching for <u>enemies</u> or danger. They do not pay attention to what they are eating because they are so busy watching for danger.

Male squirrels keep themselves very clean. The male squirrel cleans himself more times than the female squirrel. He keeps cleaning himself all day long.

Be careful when you play in the park. Squirrels are beautiful to watch, but they are not safe to touch. If you try and feed one from your hand, you could get bitten. Enjoy them from a distance.

STORY QUESTIONS

1. In which season is the squirrel most active?
   a. summer   c. fall
   b. winter   d. spring

2. Using the context clues in the passage, the word *enemies* most likely means . . .
   a. friends.   c. threats.
   b. boys.   d. girls

3. The author's purpose for this passage is . . .
   a. to entertain.
   b. to inform.
   c. to tell you what a squirrel feels like.
   d. to persuade.

4. According to this passage, what would be the danger of hand feeding a squirrel?
   a. You could attract other squirrels.
   b. You could contract a disease.
   c. You will have to take him home.
   d. You might get bitten.

SPARROWS

House sparrows are often seen in a neighborhood in the city. They like to live where there are a lot of people. They do not like to live in the country.

The female looks like she is wearing a brown cap on her head. Black streaks run down her brown back.

Male house sparrows look like they are wearing gray caps on their heads. They have a black bib under their chin, just like a baby. They have a rusty brown body. Black streaks run down the back of the male house sparrow.

Vacant lots which have dried plants or tree limbs are the perfect place for house sparrows. They love to build their nests in old trees or in empty corners. House sparrows nibble seeds that they find in the weeds or grass.

They may make nests with string or paper. These little birds pull and tear the paper. They weave it in with sticks. They love to stop and eat food out of bird feeders that hang on balconies. House sparrows will also take baths in birdbaths that people put out in front of their apartments or buildings.

<u>Keep your eyes peeled</u> if you live in the city. Chances are, you might see a house sparrow parading past!

STORY QUESTIONS

1. What is the main idea of this passage?
   a. to teach you how house sparrows eat
   b. to teach you the life span of a house sparrow
   c. to teach you to identify a sparrow in the city
   d. to teach you how to keep house like a sparrow

2. Where do house sparrows **NOT** live?
   a. in vacant lots   c. in nests made in dried plants
   b. in the city   d. in the country

3. The author's purpose for this passage is . . .
   a. to inform.   c. to entertain.
   b. to persuade.   d. to make you sad.

4. In the text above, "keep your eyes peeled" means . . .
   a. watch carefully.
   b. make sure you wear make-up on your eyes.
   c. use a potato peeler.
   d. pay attention on rainy days.

DAILY Name _____ Date _____
Warm-Up 3

HUMMINGBIRDS

Hummingbirds are amazing birds for many reasons. They fly like helicopters: backwards or floating in the air. They move from side to side. The hummingbirds zoom straight up into the sky or dive straight down. They spin their wings in circles. If their babies are in danger, they will even attack eagles. To build nests, they will pick fuzz off your sweater.

When they are awake, hummingbirds spend most of their day eating food. Hummingbirds are always on a quest for insects to eat. They need them for protein. Hummingbirds are always looking for objects from which to drink juice. They fly into brightly-colored objects that they think are food. Sometimes they even try to get juice from stop signs! They also drink nectar from flowers. Every day they visit up to 1,000 flowers to drink the juice!

Hummingbirds have special tongues. The fronts of their tongues are split in half. They have sharp edges. These edges help soak up juice from flowers. Their tongues lick flowers. As they hunt for insects, this tongue grabs the bugs and insects quickly.

Tongues, flying, and eating habits are just three of the things that make the hummingbird an unbelievable creature.

STORY QUESTIONS

1. According to the passage, what is one reason why hummingbirds are amazing?
  a. They make a great deal of noise.
  b. They are very small and delicate.
  c. They can fly like a helicopter.
  d. They can drink water.

2. In the text, "a quest for insects" means . . .
  a. questions about.   c. journey.
  b. ability.   d. search.

3. The author's purpose for this passage is to . . .
  a. entertain the reader with interesting hummingbird characteristics.
  b. inform the reader about dangerous hummingbirds.
  c. persuade the reader to purchase a hummingbird.
  d. encourage the reader to keep insects in their garden.

4. Which group of words best describes a hummingbird?
  a. never moves   c. extremely slow
  b. constantly moving   d. enjoys meat and vegetables

CAT MYTHS

People believe things about cats that might not be true. These "myths" can confuse cat owners. If you like cats, learn the facts and fiction about them.

Some people think that cats need to drink milk. That is not true. <u>If a cat eats a good diet</u>, it does not need to drink milk. Does your cat drink milk? Most cats like milk, but it can make them sick. Cats should only have milk in small amounts.

Have you heard the one about garlic? People put garlic on cat food. They believe it will get rid of worms in the cat's body. Does it work? Garlic makes food taste richer. Garlic does nothing to worms. It will give the cat bad breath! If your cat has worms, take it to an animal doctor. A veterinarian can give medicine to the cat. The medicine will take care of the worms.

Some people think that cats' whiskers help them to balance. Whiskers serve as "feelers." They do nothing at all for balance. "Feelers" help the cat know about its surroundings.

Have you heard these myths before? Do not believe them. Learn how to care for cats. Read books and talk to your veterinarian. Cats need good owners to care for them.

STORY QUESTIONS

1. According to the passage, what is the meaning of "if a cat eats a good diet"?
  a. getting the treats it deserves
  b. getting the right kind and amount of food to make them healthy
  c. getting the right kind of love and attention
  d. getting your neighbor to feed your cat while you are on vacation

2. "Cat Myths" is mostly about. . .
  a. creating a positive atmosphere for your cat.
  b. stories that are true about cats.
  c. stories that are not true about cats.
  d. making sure you have dinner in time for your cat.

3. A new title for this passage might be . . .
  a. "The Truth About Cats."   c. "Blame It on the Cat."
  b. "A Cat's Life."   d. "Safety for Cats."

4. When someone tells you new information about any topic, you should always . . .
  a. read a book that gives you advice on friendship.
  b. watch a TV show about chickens.
  c. search the Internet for video games about cats.
  d. check to see if the information is correct.

Name _____ Date _____

RATS

If you want to keep rats out of your house, there are a number of important things to remember.

First, pet food and pet dishes should be removed. When your pet is finished eating, take the dish away. Pet dishes that are outside attract rats. If you have to leave pet dishes outside, make sure they are <u>properly sanitized</u>.

Second, all trash should be put inside trashcans. Metal and heavy plastic cans are good places for trash. Make sure to close the lid. Trash should never be left in the yard. Remember to pick it up right away. Put it in the can and close the lid tightly. Trash blowing around the yard will bring unwanted furry creatures to visit.

Keep bird feeders on raised stands. Rats can eat birdseed that is close to the ground. Also, pile up any pieces of wood. Wood that is stacked will keep rats from building a nest. It should be stacked at least 18 inches above the ground. Put away pipes. These are places for rats to crawl in and out of and where they may build nests.

Last, keep windows closed tightly. Make sure windowpanes are unbroken. Rats love to crawl in cracked, broken windows. If they get in, it is hard to get them out. They will dig through everything and get into anything.

Your neighborhood can be rat free if you just follow these simple steps.

STORY QUESTIONS

1. What is this passage teaching us?
   a. how to keep rats out of our yard and homes if we live in a neighborhood
   b. how to keep rats out of our yard and homes if we live in a foreign country
   c. how to keep rats out of our yard and homes if we live on the moon
   d. how to keep rats out of our yard and homes if we live in Texas

2. Why is it important to take the pet dish inside when your pet is finished eating?
   a. Pet food spoils and smells.   c. It isn't important.
   b. The dish could break outside.   d. Rats will come to eat pet food.

3. In the text, "properly sanitized" means . . .
   a. organized.   c. cleaned.
   b. paid for.   d. dirty.

4. What information could be added to the text above?
   a. Bird feeders may be placed on the ground.
   b. Remove all cans or pet bowls that may catch the rain. Rats drink rainwater.
   c. Leave yards full of rubbish and garbage piles.
   d. Cracked or broken windows should not replaced for two months.

Name _____ Date _____

ANTS

Ants are incredible creatures. Each colony has its own smell. Each of the ants in the colony knows the smell. Enemies will not be able to enter their camp without being discovered. Several types of ants have a sting to protect their nest when <u>intruders</u> turn up.

The queen ant is the only one who can lay eggs for the colony. None of the other ants can lay eggs at all.

The worker ants cannot lay eggs. They take care of newborn baby ants. They also search for food. These worker ants protect their nest from enemies. They also keep the nest <u>spick and span</u>. They take out the "trash" from the nest and place it in one area.

Slave-maker ants rob the nest of other ants. They steal the <u>pupae</u>, the cases that hold the ant eggs. Then they bring the pupae back to their camp. When the stolen cases hatch, these stolen ants become slaves.

Finally, all ants have antennas and jaws. They need antennas for smelling and touching. They have strong, long jaws. They open and shut sideways like pairs of scissors. Adult ants cannot chew and swallow food, so they squeeze the food until the juice comes out. They swallow the juice and throw away the leftover dried parts of the food.

Ant colonies must have worker ants and slave-maker ants. They must also have a queen ant to lay eggs. They must have a way to catch other ants that try to get into their nest. Without a queen to lay eggs, or antennas to hear and touch, and jaws to tear food, there would be no ant colonies left in the world.

STORY QUESTIONS

1. According to the text, what are *pupae*?
 a. the cases that hold the ant eggs
 b. baby ants
 c. adult ants
 d. worker ants

2. Using the context above, another word for *intruders* would be . . .
 a. unwanted friends.
 b. unwanted vacationers.
 c. unwanted enemies.
 d. unwanted slaves.

3. This passage is about . . .
 a. ants going to war.
 b. unusual qualities of the ant.
 c. ants and their hobbies.
 d. how ants take out the trash.

4. Which words could be used instead of "spick and span" in the text above?
 a. sluggish and lazy
 b. dirty and piggish
 c. disgusting and awful
 d. clean and neat

Name _____ Date _____

CROWS

Crows can be a problem for farmers. They eat crops and bother farm workers. But they also do things that help farmers. Crows eat weeds, grasshoppers, wireworms, and cutworms. When crows eat these bugs and weeds, they help the farmer!

Crows are easy to spot. Most crows are black. Some are black with white, brown, or gray. Crows have black beaks and black legs. They are usually between 8 and 12 inches (20 to 30 cm) long. Their wings are between 16 and 24 inches (40 to 60 cm) wide.

Crows can be friendly with other crows. Adults enjoy being together. In the fall, crows fly south to warm weather. This is called migrating. When they <u>migrate</u>, they fly with many other crows.

Crows build nests in trees, bushes, or on the tops of buildings. They make their nests by weaving twigs together like a mat. Crows use roots, grasses, and bark from the trees to put inside of the nest. This makes the nest soft for the baby crows.

The female crow lays between four and seven eggs. They are blue-green in color. The male crow sits on the eggs. He helps to keep them warm until they hatch. When crows have babies, they like to be alone. After the babies are older, the crows will mix with other crows again.

How can you keep crows away from places? Some people make scarecrows to frighten them away. The scarecrows are made to look like people. They blow in the wind to look like people are moving. Scarecrows left to stand in one place will not work. The crows think of them as a place to land or sit. Crows are <u>quick-witted</u>. They can tell when a trap has been set.

Some people dislike crows. Others like the black, shiny birds.

STORY QUESTIONS

1. In the passage, *migrate* means . . .
   a. flying to Florida.
   b. flying to Alaska.
   c. flying south for warm weather.
   d. flying north for warm weather.

2. The words "quick-witted" could be changed to . . .
   a. speedy flyers.
   b. slow thinkers.
   c. fast thinkers.
   d. quick artists.

3. The author's purpose for writing this passage is . . .
   a. to persuade the reader to look at crows in a new way.
   b. to inform the reader about building a nest.
   c. to entertain the reader with jokes about crows.
   d. to warn the reader about dangerous birds.

4. According to this passage, how do crows help farmers?
   a. They are intelligent and quick-witted.
   b. They know that scarecrows cannot harm them.
   c. They build large, bulky nests.
   d. They eat weeds and bugs.

Name _____ Date _____

HORSES

Did you know horses are in the same family as donkeys, zebras, and mules? It is true. Horses are in the equus family. Their name comes from a Greek word. It means quick.

There are over 350 kinds of horses. They are divided into four main groups: the "light" horses, the "heavy" horses, ponies, and wild or semi-wild horses.

"Light" horses have small bones. They weigh less than 1,300 pounds (590 kg). They have thin legs.

"Heavy" horses are strong and have big bones. They also have sturdy legs. "Heavy horses" can weigh up to 2,000 pounds (907 kg).

Ponies are no taller than 58 inches (147 cm). If you measure in horse language, one would measure in hands. Ponies, then, are no more than 14 ½ hands tall.

Wild or semi-wild horses have not been tamed. These horses do not live with people. They live in the open fields and run free.

A person can tell the age of a horse by checking its teeth. Its age can only be checked by its teeth before it is ten years old.

All horses have small stomachs. They must eat small amounts of food throughout the day. All horses love to eat short, juicy grass. Horses that live outside will nibble grass all day. If they live in a stable, they will munch on hay as often as it is given to them. If they are workhorses, they will eat better if the person feeding them gives them maize (corn), oats, or barley. It can be added to their regular food. They also enjoy treats.

All horses love to run, canter, gallop, walk, or trot.

STORY QUESTIONS

1. How many main groups of horses are there?
   a. 5   b. 340   c. 4   d. 350

2. Which animals are related to the horse?
   a. mules, donkeys, and zebras   c. donkeys, zebras, and chickens
   b. mules, zebras, and cows   d. zebras, alligators, cows

3. What do all of the horses have in common?
   a. They all eat hay from the stables.
   b. They have small stomachs and eat throughout the day.
   c. They all weigh more than 1,300 pounds.
   d. They all have teeth that are 10 years old.

4. Which of these is **NOT** a fact about horses from the passage?
   a. "Heavy" horses weigh more than "light" horses.
   b. Horses belong to the equus family.
   c. They all live to be 25 years or older.
   d. Horses love short, juicy grass.

Name _____ Date _____

INTERESTING BIRD

Do you like to walk through the park early in the morning? If you do, you might see an interesting bird. It has black and white marks on its face. It has a black and white tail.

This bird might pretend to make the sound of a hawk. It might steal wasp eggs from a wasp nest. It might bury an acorn in the ground. It might nibble on acorns or nuts. It might gobble seeds found on the ground.

You could see it chasing grasshoppers, caterpillars, lizards, frogs, or other small animals. If you are lucky, you might see this bird catching an insect as it flies in the air. Zip! Zap! Goodbye, bug!

During your walk, this bird might be sitting on the trees or shrubs. This bird could be running to and fro on the ground.

Its blue-green spotted eggs will be hidden in its nest. If you see the nest, you will see twigs, little pieces of bark, leaves, and trash. The nest will probably be hidden in a corner of a building. It might be in an old, broken crate. Or finally, it might be hidden as high as thirty feet up in a tree.

What is the mystery bird? Take a walk in the park. You might see the blue jay!

STORY QUESTIONS

1. From this passage, we can conclude that the blue jay is . . .
   a. a very busy bird.
   b. a lazy bird.
   c. an angry bird.
   d. a bird with a schedule.

2. In this passage, the author describes . . .
   a. the states where blue jays live.
   b. how the baby birds learn to fly.
   c. blue jays taking a bath.
   d. the blue jay's nest.

3. The author's purpose for this passage is . . .
   a. to entertain the reader with the tricks blue jays play on people.
   b. to inform the reader so they can identify the blue jay.
   c. to persuade the reader to go to the park in search of crows.
   d. to help the reader build a birdhouse.

4. If you wished to locate more information on the blue jay, which resource would be useful?
   a. a TV show on birds of the Amazon rainforest
   b. a pamphlet on urban (city) birds
   c. a book about whales
   d. a radio show on animals of the sea

DAILY Warm-Up 10

Name _____ Date _____

DUCKS

When I think about ducks, I picture my mother's pets. She saved Lucy and Fran from a swampy area when I was 16 years old. The little ducks were weak and sick. My mother helped them to get healthy.

Lucy and Fran lived in a large cardboard box in the garage. They became family pets. They were members of our family. Lucy followed me around. She quacked and quacked. She liked attention.

My brother Tim read everything he could find about ducks. He learned to care for our pets. He made sure that the box in the garage was fit for our pets. It had a heat lamp and a feeder. He gave them water, shavings, and fresh straw each day. What a hit! Lucy and Fran loved their house. They quacked to say, "Thank you!"

One rainy morning, Lucy waddled near me to the mailbox. She walked so close we bumped into each other. I tumbled into a gigantic mud puddle. All the letters from the mailbox got wet and soggy. They dripped with muddy, brown water.

To make things worse, Tim watched from the window. When I got back into the house, he was on the kitchen floor holding the sides of his stomach. He roared with laughter.

I stomped my feet and threw up my arms. My mom calmly listened to me shout and carry on.

"It's okay, honey. If you prefer to splash in puddles, you can trade beds with the ducks!" she comforted.

With that in mind, I went to the garage and made my peace with the ducks. My own bed looked a lot better than their shavings and heat lamp.

STORY QUESTIONS

1. What is the name of the author's little brother?
   a. Tim   b. Honey   c. Mom   d. Sam

2. The story "Ducks" is mostly about a . . .
   a. boy's journey to save two ducks.   c. mother's love for animals.
   b. person's adventure with two ducks.   d. family's adventure with ducks on vacation.

3. The author's purpose for this passage is . . .
   a. to inform the reader about mistakes people make while caring for ducks.
   b. to inform the reader about the proper care and feeding of ducks.
   c. to persuade the reader to buy a pet duck.
   d. to entertain the reader with a story from the past.

4. To properly care for ducks, you should get . . .
   a. a feeder, a large cardboard box, newspaper clippings, and a heat lamp.
   b. fresh water, a large cardboard box, and a heat lamp.
   c. a box of band aids, fresh water, a large cardboard box, shavings, and a heat lamp.
   d. a stuffed animal, fresh water, a miniature cardboard box, shavings, and a heat lamp.

RACCOONS

Raccoons are cute and clever. People love their little masked faces and their comical antics. Raccoons can solve problems, and they can make messes. A raccoon can open the lid on a trashcan. Some have even opened entire garage doors!

Raccoons live in forests. They climb trees and live in nests in tree trunks. They can fish and hunt for food. Raccoons also live in cities and near homes. They live in parks and backyards. They travel through waterways and eat trash.

People should carefully wrap trash that contains food. Raccoons feast on scraps of bread, vegetables, meats, and sweets. Put these "treats" in tied plastic bags and put the bags in a strong trashcan. Make sure the lid is tight, or a raccoon might snack at your house this evening!

Raccoons are messy. They scatter food scraps, paper, cans, and other trash in yards and other areas. Would you like to clean up after a raccoon?

Raccoons played a part in history. Pictures of pioneer men wearing raccoon skin hats are often found in history books. Daniel Boone and Davy Crockett wore them. The caps kept heads warm and protected them from being scratched by branches.

Raccoons look sweet, but beware. People think they are cuddly, but raccoons are wild animals. Raccoons are dangerous. They have sharp teeth and claws. They can carry diseases. Never approach a wild raccoon. They are cute, but they are not pets.

STORY QUESTIONS

1. Where do raccoons live?
   a. only in forests
   b. only near people
   c. neither in forests nor near people
   d. in forests and near people

2. What are some of the negative things raccoons do?
   a. They damage property and shred paper.
   b. They can open your lids and doors.
   c. They tear trash out of cans.
   d. All of the above.

3. If you gave the passage a new title, it could be . . .
   a. "Battle Over Raccoons."
   b. "Keeping Your Own Raccoon."
   c. "How to Care for a Raccoon of Your Own."
   d. "Raccoons Are Clever but Dangerous."

4. Raccoon hats were worn by . . .
   a. pilgrims.
   b. cowboys.
   c. pioneers.
   d. pirates.

DAILY Warm-Up 12

Name _____ Date _____

MILKING COWS

Cows first came to America in 1611. Each farming family usually kept its own cow. A family member would milk the cow each day. It gave them milk to drink. They had to milk the cows by hand. The milk then was boiled in a big pot over the fire. It then had to cool, and after that someone skimmed the cream off the top of the pan.

Dairy farmers raise and milk cows for us. For hundreds of years, farmers spent many hours milking. Farmers, or their family members, sat on stools to squeeze milk from the cows' udders. This chore was time consuming and tiring.

Today's farmers use machines to help with milking. They can milk many cows at one time. The machines often do a better job milking than a person could.

These modern machines have long, clear hoses. The hoses carry milk to big metal tanks. The tanks hold and clean the milk. These machines help farmers milk enough cows for us all to have milk in our homes.

STORY QUESTIONS

1. According to the passage, what has improved over time?
   a. Farmers can milk cows much faster.
   b. Farmers can run faster.
   c. Farmers can plow fields faster.
   d. Farmers can drive tractors faster.

2. The main idea of the last paragraph is . . .
   a. all cows chew their cud.
   b. cows have four digestive compartments.
   c. cows make wonderful household pets.
   d. modern equipment helps farmers.

3. The first cow arrived in America in . . .
   a. 1610.   b. 1612.   c. 1611.   d. 1832.

4. What is the main idea of the passage?
   a. learning to care for a cow
   b. how technology has changed milking cows
   c. how to search for information about cows
   d. how to plan an interview with a farmer

DAILY Warm-Up 13

Name _____

Date _____

PIGS

Pigs are misunderstood. Some people think of them as lazy and stupid. Did you know that pigs are very smart? Pigs are smarter than most pets and wild animals. Experts claim that pigs are easier to train than dogs and cats. Would you want a pig for a pet?

Keeping a pet pig is fun, but it is work. Pigs like to go for walks like a dog. Would you like to walk a pig down your street? They can be trained to do tricks, and they like to be petted. They usually get along with other pets.

Pet pigs must be kept on a diet. They like to eat like hogs! An adult pet pot-bellied pig should not weigh more than 150 pounds. But many weigh up to 300 pounds due to overfeeding.

Do you sweat like a pig? Real pigs don't sweat. They cool their bodies by rolling in mud. Yet, pigs are some of the cleanest animals on the earth. Pigs can learn to use a litter box like a cat. They can be housetrained. Many live in houses and apartments. But they can get in the way.

Pigs have a keen sense of smell. They help find truffles in the forests. These mushroom-like plants sell for high prices. So the pigs are valued for their work.

In addition to ham, bacon, and pork, pigs provide us with many useful products. Pig hair is used to make hairbrushes and furniture. Drugs and medical procedures use pig parts to help sick people.

Pigs are found in every part of the world. They serve many useful purposes. Some pigs even dig holes for plant seeds to fall into and grow. Pigs may have been the world's first farmers!

STORY QUESTIONS

1. According to the text, pigs make good pets because . . .
   a. they like to watch television.
   b. you can ride a pig.
   c. they are smart and clean companions.
   d. they chase cats.

2. Pigs are found . . .
   a. throughout the entire world.
   b. throughout Europe.
   c. on tropical islands.
   d. in America and Australia.

3. Pet pot-bellied pigs should not weigh more than . . .
   a. 300 pounds.
   b. 150 pounds.
   c. 50 pounds.
   d. 500 pounds.

4. The author's purpose for writing this passage is . . .
   a. to entertain the reader with pig tales.
   b. to persuade the reader to buy pig products.
   c. to persuade the reader to get a pet pig.
   d. to inform the reader about the many qualities of pigs.

DAILY Name _____ Date _____
Warm-Up 14

HERDING DOGS

Did you know that herding dogs come in many shapes and sizes? Some are tall. Some are short. Some are lean, and some are stocky. The shortest herding dogs are Welsh corgis. These little dogs were bred to herd cattle. Their short legs move quickly when they run around the herd, and their short, little bodies can avoid a kick from an angry cow.

Most herding dogs are medium-sized. The border collie is famous for its intelligence. These dogs are active and always moving. They look for cues from the shepherd, and they work as a team. Border collies could almost work alone. They know what to do if a sheep strays.

Large dogs, like German shepherds and Belgian sheepdogs, work many jobs. They can herd, but more often they work with police, guide the blind, or provide protection to families.

Herding dogs are also trained for search and rescue work. Any time there is a disaster, you will see teams of dogs working to find missing people. Herding dogs are some of the best workers, because they are strong and determined.

Today, most dogs don't work in the jobs they were bred to do. People love them as pets. However, if given a chance, a herding dog might try to round up, or herd, the entire family. The desire to round up the group is in its blood.

STORY QUESTIONS

1. Which breed is the shortest herding dog?
   a. Shetland sheepdog   c. puli
   b. Welsh corgi   d. collie

2. The border collie is a good pet for someone who . . .
   a. likes to lounge on the couch all evening.
   b. doesn't have a backyard.
   c. is active and enjoys taking the dog on long walks.
   d. worries about dog hair on the sofa.

3. How has the job of the herding dog changed over the years?
   a. All are trained as search and rescue dogs.
   b. Some owners take their dogs to the beach.
   c. Some have become pets and are no longer trained to perform traditional jobs.
   d. They make great babysitters.

4. Which job would **NOT** be good for a herding dog?
   a. retrieving ducks from a pond   c. locating a lost hiker in the mountains
   b. working with a police officer   d. rounding up a herd of cattle

SHEEP

If you are wearing a warm, wooly sweater, thank a sheep. Wool from sheep's coats have been knit, woven, and sewn into products for many centuries. Wool is soft and warm. It resists fire and can be easily stored.

People make sweaters, clothing, blankets, rugs, carpets, and even mattresses for beds from wool. The natural fibers are washed, dyed, and combed to make yarn.

Sheep need very little care. They can climb rocks without falling. They can go for long periods without water. They eat wood and shrubs, which can be found anywhere.

Sheep are raised in one of two ways. Some sheep live in fenced pastures. Farmers provide food and water every day. Other sheep are more independent. They live on land that is owned by the farmer. They roam the grounds and find food for themselves.

Some sheep are still wild. The largest of the wild sheep live in Siberia. They are four feet (1.2 meters) tall at the shoulder. Wild sheep have enemies. Wolves and coyotes hunt sheep. Diseases and insects can make sheep sick.

Today, more than 800 breeds and varieties of sheep exist. There are five main groups of sheep. They are grouped by their fleece (wool) types. They are fine wool, long wool, crossbred wool, medium wool, and coarse wool.

People value sheep for their wool, and for meat and fat. Meat from sheep is called mutton. It is used in stews and other dishes. Fat from sheep can be made into candles and soap.

STORY QUESTIONS

1. Why are sheep important to people?
a. They are cute pets.
b. Sheep can cut your grass.
c. Sheep provide wool, meat, and fats.
d. Counting sheep helps people sleep.

2. What is sheep meat called?
a. mutton
b. steak
c. pork
d. beef

3. What product made of sheep fat can be burned in your home?
a. soap
b. a candle
c. carpet
d. paper

4. The main idea of this passage is . . .
a. to entertain the reader with funny sheep jokes.
b. to inform the reader about the many things sheep contribute to our lives.
c. to persuade the reader to sheep sit.
d. to inform the reader about things to look for when buying sheep.

DAILY Name _____ Date _____
Warm-Up 16

GOATS

Would you like a goat for a pet? Think about several things before you answer. Make sure you know the facts about any pet before you take it home.

Do you think of goats as farm animals? Goats give milk, wool, and other products. They are valuable farm animals. But they can be great pets, too.

Think of goats in petting zoos. They are friendly and curious. People like to pet the goats and watch them play. Pet goats are liked for the same reasons. Some breeds, such as the dwarf or pygmy goats, are small enough to keep in a house with a yard. But goats have some special needs.

Goats are herd animals, so they like to live in groups. A pair of goats would please the right family. Goats can also live with horses. Rural areas are best suited for keeping goats. Goats need your time and attention. They need medical care.

Goats love you to brush their coats. They love when you touch their ears. A goat has sharp teeth, so remember to keep your hands out if its mouth. A vet must trim your goat's hooves.

A female goat is called a nanny goat. It is also called a doe. A male goat is called a billy goat. He is also called a buck. The baby goat is called a kid.

Goats are picky eaters. Goats love molasses, carrots, and seaweed meal. These are very good for them. Crushed oats, pony pellets, bran, chaff, horse mix, Lucerne hay, and crushed oats are also foods they that they will enjoy eating. Goats love to eat fresh roots from young trees most of all.

If you want to keep a goat for a pet, prepare for its needs. Then your goat will be happy and so will you.

STORY QUESTIONS

1. Which statement is **TRUE**?
   a. Goats do not need other animals.
   b. Goats have dull teeth.
   c. A female goat is called a kid.
   d. Goats can give milk.

2. Goats like to be in groups because . . .
   a. they are herd animals.
   b. they like the heat.
   c. they cannot see.
   d. they get lost easily.

3. The author's purpose for this passage is . . .
   a. to entertain the reader with a goat story.
   b. to inform the reader about goat tricks.
   c. to inform the reader about goat facts, in case they wish to purchase one for a pet.
   d. to persuade the reader to start a goat farm.

4. What is something you should **NOT** do if you have goat for a pet?
   a. Feed it pony pellets.
   b. Brush it.
   c. Put your hand in its mouth.
   d. Feed it carrots.

Name _____ Date _____

GEESE

Geese fly south for the winter. They fly as a group, in a V shape. This shape is called a formation. Why do they fly in formations?

As each bird flaps its wings, the wind it makes lifts the bird that follows behind. The geese gather lift from one another. This helps the geese travel faster. They work as a team.

If one of the geese falls out of the V, it will feel the pull from flying alone. It will want to come right back to the V.

The goose that is in the front of the V will drop to the back when it gets tired. Another goose takes over leading the birds. The geese behind the leader make honking noises. The noise encourages the lead birds as they fly along. The honking makes the birds keep up the speed. By honking, birds tell each other, "Good job. Keep it up!"

If a goose gets injured or sick, it falls out of the V. Two other geese from the group follow it down to the ground. They help or protect the bird. These two geese stay with the bird until it dies or is able to fly again. If the bird dies, they wait for another flock and join in their V. If the bird gets better, they all join.

People can learn a lot from geese. We can work together to get jobs done. We can take turns being the leader. When someone is having a hard time, we can help. We can let others know when they are doing a good job. If we acted like the geese, wouldn't our world be a happy place?

STORY QUESTIONS

1. Why do the geese fly in a V formation?
   a. They can get where they are going faster and with less effort.
   b. They can have a better view of the world from the formation.
   c. They can travel in larger circles in a V formation.
   d. They will be able to head to vacation more quickly.

2. Which statement is **FALSE**?
   a. Geese change places when they are tired from flying in front.
   b. Geese fly in formation.
   c. Geese do not help wounded or dying geese.
   d. Geese encourage each other by honking.

3. The author's purpose for this passage is . . .
   a. to entertain the reader with geese tales.
   b. to inform the reader about lessons we can learn from the examples of geese.
   c. to persuade the reader to travel in formation with the geese.
   d. to inform the reader how to take care of a pet goose.

4. A **synonym** for *encourages* could be . . .
   a. annoys.   c. pressures.
   b. bothers.   d. supports.

DAILY Warm-Up 18   Name _____   Date _____

CHICKENS

Have you ever seen a city chicken? Some people enjoy keeping chickens as pets. Chickens are not cuddly like cats or friendly like dogs, but they do show affection.

A friendly chicken might hop on the back of your lawn chair. It could walk near you in the backyard. It might gently pull on your hair if you are lying on the grass. Chickens might even walk into your lap and eat food from your hand.

Before getting a pet chicken, think about its needs. Check to make sure that your city allows chickens to be kept as pets. Call your local animal shelter for information. Consider your neighbors. Would they mind if you kept chickens? Check your yard for size and escape paths. Chickens need exercise!

Gather the right supplies for chickens. A good chicken <u>coop</u> made of chicken wire and wood will house your pet. The coop must have a door for the chickens to pass through easily. Airtight containers keep the chicken food from getting stale or soggy. You will need clean-up supplies and nesting materials. A chicken breeder can give you a list of recommended items.

Are you ready for the responsibilities of keeping an active pet or are you "chicken"?

STORY QUESTIONS

1. Which is a **synonym** for the word *coop*?
   a. cop
   b. boring
   c. enclosure
   d. rooster

2. Before getting a pet chicken, you should think about . . .
   a. city laws, your neighbors, and pet supplies.
   b. city laws, your neighbors, and what you can do with the eggs.
   c. what the neighbors know about chickens and what they like to do.
   d. how chickens sunbathe and if your neighbors want eggs.

3. The author's purpose for this passage is . . .
   a. to entertain the reader with facts about farm chickens.
   b. to inform the reader about raising chickens in a city.
   c. to persuade the reader to stay away from chickens.
   d. to suggest a price for eggs.

4. Which could be a different title for this passage?
   a. "Caring for Chicken Pox"
   b. "Caring for Your Pet Chicken"
   c. "Chickens Gone Wild"
   d. "Playing with Chickens"

DAILY Name _____ Date _____
Warm-Up 1

DANIEL BOONE

Daniel Boone was an explorer. Many people say that he found the state of Kentucky. Daniel was born November 2, 1734. He learned farming, hunting, and other skills on the family farm. He liked to explore the woods. As a <u>youngster</u>, Daniel spent many days exploring plants and wild animals. The woods were his home.

When he turned nineteen, Daniel went into the army. He drove a supply wagon in the French and Indian War. On one <u>military expedition</u>, he met a man named John Finley. John was a great storyteller. He told Daniel many stories about travel and exploring. Daniel loved these stories. He wanted to explore, just like John.

Not long after he met John Finley, he went back to his parents' home. At this time, he married Rebecca Bryan, who was a neighbor of his parents. For a little while he stayed with Rebecca on a little farm.

But his need for adventure sent him on many trips. He traveled throughout the wilderness. He eventually helped pioneers travel and set up homes.

Throughout his life, Daniel traveled thousands of miles on foot or by horse. His dream to discover new places and new things became real. Many thrilling stories have been written about Daniel and his adventures.

STORY QUESTIONS

1. What is the meaning of the word *youngster* from the passage above?

   a. someone who is a child

   b. a young cow

   c. doctor

   d. someone who doesn't like being young

2. From the passage above, we can infer that Daniel Boone was . . .

   a. a nice man.   c. an explorer.

   b. a dogsled racer.   d. an excellent shot with a rifle.

3. Another phrase for "military expedition" would be . . .

   a. pleasure vacation.   c. presidential trip.

   b. journey with the armed forces.   d. a trip back home.

4. How did John Finley influence Daniel Boone's life?

   a. He taught him to shoot a rifle.

   b. He filled his head with information about trees and plants.

   c. He got him to camp in the woods.

   d. He always told him stories of wild, interesting adventures and travels.

DAILY Name _____ Date _____
Warm-Up 2

JOHNNY APPLESEED

Have you ever planted a seed and watched it grow? A man known as Johnny Appleseed planted millions of seeds. Apple trees across the United States trace their roots to Johnny Appleseed.

Johnny "Appleseed" was born John Chapman. He was well known because of his love for planting apple trees. He was also known for his stories. By the time he was 25, he became a nurseryman. He took care of plants and trees. Johnny planted entire orchards of apples in New York and Pennsylvania.

This gentle man walked through the wilderness. He carried a bag of apple seeds on his back. When he found a spot he felt was just right to plant, he stopped. In the clearings, he planted apple seeds in neat rows. When the planting was finished, he built a fence to keep away wild animals.

The seeds sprouted, and Appleseed sold the plants to settlers in the area. They enjoyed the fruit of these trees for years and years. Appleseed received money for the saplings, and sometimes he traded for clothes or supplies.

Appleseed always worked alone. But he made many friends along his routes. Many families welcomed him for overnight stays.

Johnny Appleseed was a simple man. He did not care about things like fancy clothes or money. He rarely wore shoes. His feet had big bumps on both sides. They looked as hard and tough as leather.

He was rough, but children loved his gentle ways. His cheerful attitude made settlers happy. Johnny left apples wherever he went. He called them his "joy" that he left behind.

STORY QUESTIONS

1. What was Johnny Appleseed's real name?
   a. John Childress
   b. John Chapman
   c. Ohio River
   d. Nicholas Sparks

2. In this passage, Johnny Appleseed is best known for his . . .
   a. way with animals.
   b. worn out clothes.
   c. nursery skills and sadness.
   d. apple trees and gentle ways.

3. The author's purpose for this passage is to . . .
   a. persuade the reader to learn more about Johnny Appleseed.
   b. entertain the reader with Johnny Appleseed stories.
   c. inform the reader about the positive way Johnny Appleseed influenced America.
   d. convince children to eat apples.

4. What conclusion could you draw about Johnny Appleseed?
   a. He had a dream, and he worked hard to make it come true.
   b. He loved to wear new clothes.
   c. Big houses and cars were important to him.
   d. He disliked people and nature a great deal.

DAILY Warm-Up 3

Name _____

Date _____

SACAGAWEA

<u>Sacagawea</u> means "Bird Woman." She was a Native American guide who led the Lewis and Clark expedition across the United States. The trip started in St. Louis, Missouri, and ended at the Pacific Ocean.

Sacagawea was the daughter of a Shoshone Indian chief. She was born in the year 1790. When she was ten years old, her village was raided. All of the homes were set on fire. She was taken prisoner by the Hidatsa Indians.

Sacagawea was traded from one tribe to another. The princess became a slave. One day, natives were gambling with a French Canadian trapper. His name was Toussaint Charbonneau. He won the game, and Sacagawea was his prize. She became one of his many wives. She was just sixteen.

Sacagawea could speak many languages. She understood many Native American dialects. This made her very valuable. When Lewis and Clark asked Charbonneau to be their interpreter on a trip, they also asked for Sacagawea to come along. They felt she would be valuable as an interpreter, but also as a guide. Lewis and Clark also felt she would be a good sign of peace to Native Americans they met along the way.

Sacagawea had other valuable skills. She was strong and hard working. She helped Lewis and Clark pick plants for food. She taught them the ways of the Native Americans to help them survive in the wilderness. Sacagawea had a son who was born while they traveled. She continued to lead the trip.

Sacagawea helped many of the men through hard times. More than once she saved explorers from drowning in the rivers. She made them laugh and treated them kindly. Without her, the Lewis and Clark expedition would not have had success.

STORY QUESTIONS

1. What was Sacagawea's childhood like?
a. She lived in her own village for her entire life.
b. She was traded as a slave and learned several Native American languages.
c. She had many friends and participated in fun activities.
d. She went to school in New York.

2. Why did Sacagawea marry Toussaint Charbonneau?
a. She was the prize he won in a gambling game.
b. She wanted to marry him.
c. Her father made her marry him.
d. Her mother told her to marry him.

3. Sacagawea worked with Lewis and Clark as a . . .
a. cook.
b. housekeeper.
c. guide.
d. nanny.

4. What does *Sacagawea* mean?
a. Small Fry
b. Lewis and Clark
c. Toussaint Charbonneau
d. Bird Woman

DAILY Warm-Up 4

Name _____ **Date** _____

DAVY CROCKETT

Davy Crockett did many great things in his life. He was a frontiersman and an explorer. He became a leader in the Creek Indian War. He was later a congressman in the United States House of Representatives. Davy was born into a poor family, but he did not let that stop him from accomplishing many things.

Davy's life began in a small cabin on August 17, 1786. He was the fifth of nine children. They moved many times when he was young. At the age of 13, Davy ran away from home to avoid getting in trouble by his father. While on his own, he went from town to town and learned many skills through the jobs he took and as a hunter and trapper. After almost three years, he returned home. His his family was surprised but happy to see him. Davy worked for a year for men to whom his father owed money. Later, he was able to save his earnings and buy things for himself.

In 1806, Davy married Polly Finlay, and they had three children. She died, and he married Elizabeth Patton. She was a widow with two children.

Davy died fighting for freedom. He died at the Battle of the Alamo in Texas in 1836. Through the years, Davy has been the subject of songs, books, TV programs, and movies.

STORY QUESTIONS

1. How old was Davy Crockett when he died?

a. 46   c. 45

b. 60   d. 50

2. Why did Davy run away from home?

a. because he wanted to go live in the woods

b. because he was worried about getting in trouble

c. because he was afraid of getting married

d. because he had to work for his father

3. What conclusions can you draw about Davy Crockett?

a. He worked hard and did many important things.

b. He was lazy and didn't do much with his life.

c. He became a famous explorer.

d. He didn't like politics.

4. Which statement does **NOT** explain how Davy Crockett made our country a better place?

a. He died fighting at the Alamo.

b. He served in the House of Representatives.

c. He could hit the center of any target with his rifle.

d. He was a leader in the Creek Indian War.

NARCISSA WHITMAN

Have you ever been wrongly accused of something? Narcissa Whitman lost her life because someone lied about her. Her life was a mixture of victories and tragedies. She did things no one else could.

Narcissa was born in New York on March 14, 1808. When she was young, she loved to read. The stories of Harriet Broadman, a missionary to India, were her favorites. A missionary is someone who does religious or charitable work. The stories told of good deeds and helping others. Narcissa dreamed of becoming a missionary herself.

Narcissa became a teacher; however, she never gave up her dream of being a missionary. She tried to find a placement, but unmarried women were not accepted at that time.

Narcissa married a man named Marcus Whitman. He was a doctor and a missionary. Her dream finally became real. The day after their wedding, they headed down the dusty trail. They moved west to help others. She would share her beliefs and tend to others' needs.

For 11 years, they lived in the Oregon territory. They had one daughter, Alice. When she was two years old, Alice fell into a river and drowned. She never had any more children of her own, but the Whitmans later adopted several other children.

Even though Narcissa had dreamed of being a missionary, she didn't know what was in store for her. Life was much more difficult than she had known. For many years she was the only woman living in the mission. She missed her family and mail was slow to bring news from them.

Narcissa found it hard to understand the ways of the Native Americans. They did not understand her. In 1847, a measles outbreak took the lives of many natives, but most of the Caucasians survived. The natives claimed that the Whitmans were poisoning them and that they wanted to steal all the land. This lie caused a revolt.

The mission was destroyed. The Whitmans and others were killed. A terrible lie killed a wonderful woman and those around her.

STORY QUESTIONS

1. What was Narcissa's dream as a child?
  a. to become an artist
  b. to become a painter
  c. to become a missionary
  d. to become a settler

2. Why was she unable to become a missionary at first?
  a. She was too young.
  b. Single women were not allowed to be missionaries then.
  c. She was too old.
  d. Her mother would not let her go.

3. How was Narcissa's dream of becoming a missionary different from the real thing?
  a. She found the job to be exciting.
  b. She got to travel much more than she originally thought.
  c. She found that she had to learn to cook and clean.
  d. She found the job to be hard and lonely.

4. What type of literature is the passage above?
  a. biography
  b. historical fiction
  c. adventure
  d. fairy tale

DAILY Warm-Up 6

Name _____ Date _____

STAGECOACH MARY FIELDS

Mary Fields lived in the American Wild West. She was born a slave and became an orphan. She never married, and she had no children. This African-American woman found work in a convent in Toledo, Ohio. She formed a strong bond with Mother Amadeus.

The nuns moved to Montana, where Mother Amadeus became very ill. When Mary learned of the illness, she traveled to Montana. She nursed the nun back to health. She then stayed at the mission. Mary protected the nuns from thieves and criminals. She was a pistol-packing woman who never turned away from a fight.

She was six feet tall and as strong as any man. Mary helped build a school and carry supplies. She could fix anything! She became the foreman of the workers. Men reported to her! However, her temper got the best of her, and she was forced to leave the mission. The nuns helped her start a business nearby.

Mary opened a café. She did not make any money. Her heart was too big. She fed the hungry without pay. She could not turn away people who needed help. When the café closed, Mary found a new job.

This job suited her well. In 1895, she became a driver of a U.S. mail coach. She became the second woman—and the first African-American woman—to ever work for the post office. She and her mule, Moses, never missed a day. She earned her nickname, "Stagecoach," for her reliability. She did this job until she was 70 years old! "Stagecoach" Mary Fields broke boundaries of race, gender, and age.

STORY QUESTIONS

1. What was so unusual about Mary?
   a. She was gentle and kind.
   b. She worked at a mission.
   c. She tipped her wagon in the middle of the night.
   d. She carried a gun, was tough, and did the jobs of men in the Old West.

2. What do you think the phrase "pistol-packing" means?
   a. packing a pistol into a suitcase
   b. wrapping up a pistol as a gift
   c. carrying a pistol
   d. burying a pistol

3. What do you think would **NOT** have been part of Mary's job at the mission?
   a. carrying firewood
   b. sewing
   c. digging a well
   d. building a storage room

4. Why did Mary get the nickname "Stagecoach"?
   a. She was as reliable as a stagecoach.
   b. She was as big as a stagecoach.
   c. She was as fast as a stagecoach.
   d. She could carry a stagecoach.

DAILY
Warm-Up 7

Name _____   Date _____

CLARA BARTON

Clara Barton was America's first nurse. When she was 11, her big brother fell off a barn roof. He was badly injured. She took care of him. That is when she knew what she wanted to do with her life.

When the Civil War started, there was no such thing as a nurse! Barton decided that the hurt and dying soldiers needed care. She went right out into the battlefields to help them. She refused to rest if even one wounded man needed care. Sometimes she worked for three days straight with only one meal and an hour and a half of sleep.

Barton had one goal: she wanted to be sure that every injured soldier was properly taken care of. And nothing stopped her. She burned her hands but kept working. She got frostbite on her fingers. Still, she took care of the men. Twice she was nearly shot: one bullet passed through her sleeve, and the other tore off a part of her skirt.

After the war, she went to Europe to rest. But instead, she became a nurse to the men on the battlefields of Europe. There she heard about the Red Cross. The Red Cross gave any wounded person care and food. It did not matter what side they were on. And no one would attack a tent flying a Red Cross flag.

When she returned home, she formed the American Red Cross to meet people's needs during emergencies. The first people the American Red Cross helped were those who had lost their homes due to a big forest fire. Barton continued to work with the American Red Cross until she died at the age of 91.

STORY QUESTIONS

1. Most of the soldiers Clara cared for had been . . .
   a. burned.   c. frostbitten.
   b. shot.   d. kicked.

2. What happened last?
   a. Clara took care of men on the battlefield.
   b. Clara took care of her brother.
   c. Clara started the American Red Cross.
   d. Clara went to Europe.

3. Why did Clara form the American Red Cross?
   a. She wanted to help anyone in need.
   b. She had seen the Red Cross during the Civil War and thought it was a good idea.
   c. She wanted to fight fires.
   d. She wanted to help soldiers.

4. When Clara went into the battlefields to care for the soldiers, she showed that she was . . .
   a. scared.   c. brave.
   b. selfish.   d. wounded.

CHARLIE PARKHURST

Have you ever been tricked? Charlie Parkhurst tricked a lot of people. When Charlie died, we found out the truth—Charlie was really Charlotte!

Charlotte was born in New Hampshire around 1812. She was orphaned at an early age, and her life changed. In order to survive, Charlotte became Charlie. She escaped from an orphanage by dressing as a boy. She learned that boys could get jobs, but little girls could not. Boys could learn trades; they could make a living. So she dressed in pants and boys' things.

Charlie tried a few jobs, and "he" found his calling. Charlie worked as a stable boy. People saw that he was good with horses. This skill led to a great career. He learned to handle teams of horses. Stagecoach driving was the perfect job for him!

He could drive a stagecoach <u>plum full of</u> passengers, bags, mail, and gold dust. He would get it safely across the Sierra Nevada Mountains. For twenty years people rode safely across the mountains with Charlie. He proved that he was one of the best drivers. Everybody felt safe when they were with him.

Charlie met outlaws twice. The first time, they got the box of money. It was full. The second time, Charlie was ready for them. He made sure the bandits didn't get what they were after. The passengers watched from inside the stagecoach.

When Charlie died, the coroner found out the truth. Charlie was a woman! She had done things women never dreamed of. She'd been the best stagecoach driver in the area. She had even voted for the president of the United States 50 years before women were allowed to vote!

STORY QUESTIONS

1. Why is "he" in quotes in paragraph three?
   a. because someone said these words
   b. because "he" is really a "she"
   c. it should not have quotes
   d. because it is the title of an article

2. A group of words that could be used instead of "plum full of" in paragraph four would be . . .
   a. stuffed with.
   b. empty.
   c. full of plums.
   d. missing several.

3. Why did Charlie take a fake identity?
   a. to hide from his parents
   b. to hide from police
   c. because no girls' clothes were available
   d. to escape from an orphanage and be able to get work

4. What question would Charlie have been able to answer?
   a. How did the United States win its freedom?
   b. What do railroads keep in the engine room?
   c. How did you keep your identity a secret all of those years?
   d. How do you take care of sheep?

DAILY Name _____ Date _____
Warm-Up 9

DR. ANTONIA NOVELLO

In 1990, the U.S. Surgeon General was Dr. Antonia Novello. She was the first woman to have this job. She was the first Latina, too. The Surgeon General is the nation's main doctor. She does research. She tells the public what she finds. Novello taught about the dangers of smoking and drinking alcohol. She told the companies that make beer, wine, and cigarettes to stop trying to get teens to buy their products. She taught people how to keep from getting AIDS, too.

Novello was born in Puerto Rico. She earned a medical degree there in 1970. She always wanted to become a doctor. But she didn't know that she'd one day be the most important doctor in America.

As a child, she had a health problem. It hurt a lot. But she did not get the operation she needed until she was 18. While growing up, Novello didn't want other kids to feel sorry for her. Although she was in pain, she made jokes. She laughed a lot. She made friends with everyone. But she worked hard to earn good grades. Later she had a set of operations during medical school. Yet her grades did not fall. She always did her best.

Novello was shocked when she was asked to be Surgeon General. She wasn't looking for a new job. President George Bush spoke to her himself. So Dr. Novello took the job. She left after three years. Today she still works to improve health care for women, children, and the poor.

STORY QUESTIONS

1. Where was Dr. Novello born and raised?
   a. in Latin America   c. in Puerto Rico
   b. in South America   d. in Mexico

2. How did Dr. Novello become interested in being a doctor?
   a. She was sick as a child and knew she wanted to help others get better.
   b. The president told her that she would be a good doctor.
   c. Her mother told her that she should become a doctor.
   d. She wanted to be the U.S. Surgeon General.

3. During medical school, Dr. Novello . . .
   a. did not do her best because of her operations.
   b. was asked to be the U.S. Surgeon General.
   c. had operations yet kept her grades high.
   d. had to stop and start classes due to her illness.

4. How did Dr, Novello react when asked to be Surgeon General?
   a. She expected it.   c. She was afraid.
   b. She was shocked.   d. She was sad.

LOUIS PASTEUR

Louis Pasteur lived long ago. But the things he did help keep you healthy today. He was not a medical doctor. Yet he found new ways to help keep people from getting ill. Pasteur studied germs. He figured out that germs could live almost anywhere. He believed that these germs caused sickness.

Pasteur proved that sicknesses happen when germs get inside a body and multiply. He also found that if a few weak germs were put into an animal, the animal's body would develop its own defense against the germ. He proved this by giving sheep and chickens shots of weak germs. And it worked! Those animals no longer caught the bad sicknesses.

In 1881 he started work on a shot to stop rabies. Four years later, a rabid dog bit a boy. The parents asked Pasteur to save their son. Pasteur did not want to use his shot on a person. He was not sure what would happen. But he knew that the boy was sure to die without it. The shot was his only chance. So Pasteur gave him the first human vaccine. The little boy lived.

Pasteur wanted to come up with a way to keep germs from getting into people's bodies. He found a way to make milk free of germs. He learned that germs could not stand heat. When he heated milk to 140°F and then quickly cooled it and sealed it in clean jars, the germs died. His method is called *pasteurization*. It has been used on milk ever since. Today it is used to prevent germ growth in other products, too.

STORY QUESTIONS

1. Which of these does **NOT** describe Louis Pasteur?
   a. very smart   c. helpful
   b. great doctor   d. willing to take risks

2. What happened last?
   a. A rabid dog bit a boy.
   b. Pasteur developed a rabies shot.
   c. Pasteur gave a boy a vaccine.
   d. The parents begged Pasteur to help.

3. How does a vaccine work?
   a. It kills germs as they enter the body.
   b. It doesn't let germs get into the body.
   c. It makes the body produce more red blood cells.
   d. It helps the body make a defense against germs.

4. Why does a pasteurized liquid need to be sealed in a clean jar?
   a. to be sure that no germs are already in the jar or can get into the jar
   b. to be sure that the germs cannot get the air they need to breathe
   c. to keep the liquid at the right temperature
   d. to make the liquid taste better

DAILY Warm-Up 11

Name _____ Date _____

ELIZABETH BLACKWELL

Elizabeth Blackwell left England in 1832. She was just 11 years old when she arrived in New York City. The streets were quiet. Few people were around. Most of them were sick. They had cholera. Some even died. Those who were not sick stayed inside. They didn't want to catch it. Blackwell wanted to help the ill people get well. But she was just a girl.

She never forgot her dream of helping the sick. When she grew up, a friend fell ill. Blackwell nursed her back to health. She told her friend that she wanted to be a doctor. Her friend told her to try.

At that time, few women went to college. None had ever earned a medical degree. Blackwell studied the same books that the medical students did. She paid doctors to teach her. Soon she was ready for medical school. At first no college would let her in. It took her years to convince Geneva Medical College to let her try. Then the teachers and students were mean to her. To please the teachers, Blackwell had to work harder than the other students did. She earned high marks in each class.

In 1849, Blackwell was the first woman in the United States to graduate as a medical doctor. But then no one would hire her. No one would rent her space so that she could have her own office. Yet Blackwell did not give up. She started the Women's Medical College. There she helped other women to become doctors, too. And in 1857, she opened a hospital. She treated poor women and children. Few could pay her. But Blackwell was happy. She was helping the sick.

STORY QUESTIONS

1. Where did Blackwell go to medical school?
   a. Geneva Medical College
   b. Women's Medical College
   c. Hobart and William Smith College
   d. Peoples' Medical College

2. What did Blackwell do in 1832?
   a. earned a doctor's degree
   b. came to the U.S. from England
   c. opened her own hospital
   d. decided to go to college

3. Blackwell was most interested in giving medical care to . . .
   a. rich people.
   b. women.
   c. men.
   d. poor women and children.

4. Which statement is **NOT** true?
   a. Blackwell was the first woman in the U.S. to graduate as a doctor.
   b. Many colleges wanted Blackwell to go to school there.
   c. Blackwell opened her own hospital.
   d. Blackwell always dreamed about becoming a doctor.

DAILY
Warm-Up 12

Name _____   Date _____

CESAR CHAVEZ

Cesar Chavez was born in 1927 in Arizona. His family had come from Mexico. His father had a small store. His grandfather had a farm. But the store started to lose money. Chavez's father had to sell it. They moved to his grandfather's farm. They worked hard, but they needed money to pay taxes on the farm. If they could not pay, they would lose the farm.

Chavez's father became a migrant farm worker. Migrant farm workers move from farm to farm. They plant and pick crops. They work hard. The jobs do not last long. They are paid very little. Even though Chavez's father worked hard, he could not earn enough money to save the farm. They became homeless. Then all of them—even the children—had to work in the fields.

As migrant workers, they followed the crops. At some farms, they stayed in shacks that had no running water or electricity. At other farms, they lived in a tent. Once Chavez's family picked grapes. But when the job was done, the farmer would not pay them! There was nothing they could do. They went to the next farm.

When Chavez grew up, he wanted to change things for migrant workers. He formed the United Farm Workers (UFW). This union wanted better pay and housing for farm workers. Chavez fasted. He would not eat. This made the TV and newspapers tell his story. People were shocked when they heard about the problems of migrant workers. They made the largest growers sign contracts with the UFW. Then Chavez started to eat again.

Another time he stopped eating because of pesticides. They were sprayed on crops. They were harming farm workers. He did not eat until the farmers stopped using the bad chemicals.

STORY QUESTIONS

1. How did the Chavez family lose their farm?
   a. They could not pay the taxes on the farm.
   b. The did not work hard.
   c. Someone stole all of their money.
   d. All of their crops died.

2. What did Chavez do when he fasted?
   a. He only ate at night.
   b. He refused to eat food.
   c. He ate less food than usual.
   d. He ate more food than usual.

3. Why did Chavez form the UFW?
   a. to get free healthcare for migrant workers
   b. to improve schools for migrant workers
   c. to be the leader of the migrant workers
   d. to get better housing and pay for migrant workers

4. One reason Chavez fasted is because . . .
   a. he wanted farm workers to all wear uniforms.
   b. he wanted to be famous and on TV.
   c. he wanted farmers to stop using bad chemicals on crops.
   d. he wanted farmers to stop growing extra crops.

DAILY
Warm-Up 13

Name _____ Date _____

CALAMITY JANE

Calamity Jane lived in the Old West. Born on May 1, 1852, her real name was Martha Cannary. She loved horses more than anything else. She rode them without being afraid. When she was 13 years old, her family moved from Missouri to Montana. They traveled by covered wagon. The trip took five months. Traveling gave her a lot of time to shoot her rifle and ride her horse.

Martha decided she wanted to join the army. She worked for General Custer as a scout at a fort in Wyoming. Her job was to ride ahead of the army and then tell them what she saw. She had to make sure it was safe to travel.

Martha had always worn dresses. Her job as a scout changed that. She had to wear a soldier's uniform with men's pants. Martha felt strange at first. But the more she wore them, the more she liked them. Pants made it easier to ride a horse, and they were more comfortable.

One day she and a captain of the army were sent to stop a fight between different Native American groups. They took other soldiers with them to help out too. When they were coming back, they were <u>ambushed</u> from behind. Martha turned around just in time to see the captain get shot and fall off his horse. Martha turned, scooped him up, and put him on her horse. She held him as they rode back to the army post. When the captain was better, he laughed and said, "I name you, Calamity Jane, heroine of the plains!"

STORY QUESTIONS

1. *Ambushed* is another word for . . .
   a. laughed at.
   b. spit on.
   c. a surprise attack.
   d. called names.

2. Why was Martha named "heroine of the plains"?
   a. She saved the life of a captain in an unusual, dangerous way.
   b. She could ride horses very fast.
   c. She was an excellent shot with a rifle.
   d. She rode to scout out the territory.

3. The author's purpose for this passage is to . . .
   a. inform the reader about Custer's last stand.
   b. inform the reader about how Martha became Calamity Jane.
   c. inform the reader about travels in the Wild West.
   d. inform the reader about how Calamity Jane died.

4. Martha began to wear men's clothing when . . .
   a. her father died.
   b. her mother died.
   c. her dresses no longer fit.
   d. she became a scout.

SALLY RIDE

Sally Ride was an astronaut. She was the first American woman to travel into space. She left Earth on June 18, 1983. She came back on June 24th. She traveled with four other astronauts in the spaceship *Challenger*.

Challenger orbited Earth. When something orbits something, it goes around it. How long did it take *Challenger* to orbit Earth? It took only 90 minutes! *Challenger* orbited Earth 16 times in just one day. This meant that Ride saw the sun rise and set 16 times in one day!

Ride liked being an astronaut. She liked being in space. She liked how it felt when the force of gravity was not pulling her down. Without the force of gravity, she could float. She floated from place to place. While in space, she played a game to catch jellybeans. The jellybeans were floating, too! Ride had to catch the jellybeans with her mouth!

Sally Ride worked hard to become an astronaut. She went to school for many years. She had to have special training. The training was hard work. Ride was a good astronaut. She went into space two times. Ride then became a teacher. She wrote books and helped direct space research. When you research something, you study it. You try to find out new things about it. Sally Ride received several awards and honors for her work and continues to be committed to science education.

STORY QUESTIONS

1. This story is mainly about . . .
   a. spaceships.
   b. a woman astronaut.
   c. space travel.
   d. astronaut training.

2. What statement is **true**?
   a. Sally Ride wrote books in space.
   b. Sally Ride did not like being an astronaut.
   c. Sally Ride went into space two times.
   d. Sally Ride liked the force of gravity in space.

3. If you wanted to find out more about space travel, you might _____ it.
   a. research   c. travel
   b. orbit   d. float

4. How long was Ride in space the first time?
   a. 6 days   c. 4 days
   b. 8 days   d. 16 days

ANNIE OAKLEY

Annie Oakley was born in Ohio on August 13, 1860. Her parents were poor Quakers who lived on a small farm. Annie learned to trap animals and do chores. In 1866, her father died. When she was eight, her mom sent her to work for a neighbor. She learned to embroider and sew from the neighbor's wife.

After two years, she ran away. Annie came back to the farm. Her family could not pay the bills and did not have money to pay for the farm. Annie went to work, hunting animals to sell to restaurants and hotels. She was very good at trapping animals, and she could shoot well. Soon she earned enough money to buy the family farm.

People heard stories about Annie and her gun. The manager of one of the hotels was in charge of a shooting contest. He asked Annie to enter the contest. She and her brother saved $50.00 to enter the contest. Annie won the contest by one shot. She beat a famous shooter named Frank Butler. He could not believe how well she could shoot a gun. He asked her to marry him, and she did.

Annie and Frank spent 15 years acting in Wild West shows. Annie Oakley was a great actress. She was the star of the show. Frank was her manager. She could shoot a hole in a card from ninety feet away. She could shoot an apple off her dog's head. She could even shoot a cigarette out of Frank's mouth! Annie could shoot faster than any man for miles around.

STORY QUESTIONS

1. What was Annie's childhood like?
   a. interesting and full of adventures
   b. easy and fun
   c. very difficult and full of hard work
   d. gentle and proper

2. From the passage, it is safe to guess that . . .
   a. Annie had a good education.
   b. Annie trusted herself with a gun.
   c. Annie loved to clean house.
   d. Annie was lazy.

3. Annie showed us that . . .
   a. riding horses was a good skill to have.
   b. if you want something bad enough, you will work hard to get it.
   c. acting was the best choice of careers.
   d. none of the above.

4. We know that Annie cared about her family because . . .
   a. she taught her sisters to embroider.
   b. she read to her family.
   c. she made enough money to buy the farm for her family.
   d. she trapped with her brother.

Name _____ Date _____

DALE EVANS

Have you seen Dale Evans on television? She starred in movies and television shows. She was in more than 28 old-time cowboy movies. Dale was also a singer.

Some say her real name is Frances Octavia Smith. Others claim it was Lucille Wood Smith. What we do know is that her life began in Uvalde, Texas. She ran away with her high school sweetheart to get married when she was only fourteen. They moved to Tennessee and had a baby boy named Tom. One year later her husband died.

Frances/Lucille found a job at a radio station. She sang and played the piano. The manager of the station changed her name to Dale Evans. The name was catchy. It stayed with her.

Dale moved to Chicago and then back to Texas. She was hired as an actress and singer. On the set of one of her movies, she met a famous cowboy actor. His name was Roy Rogers. They made many movies as a team. They liked the same things. They became best friends. One year later they were married at the ranch where they made their first movie.

Roy and Dale shared a happy life. They were loved by all of America.

STORY QUESTIONS

1. Why did Frances/Lucille run away?
   a. She wanted to get married.
   b. She wanted to get a job.
   c. She did not like school.
   d. She always ran away.

2. Which of the following is **NOT** a fact about Dale Evans?
   a. She had a job at a radio station.
   b. She went by the name Annie Oakley.
   c. She played the piano.
   d. She starred in movies.

3. Dale met Roy Rogers . . .
   a. at a baseball game.
   b. on a movie set.
   c. at a park.
   d. at the zoo.

4. Roy and Dale were a good match because . . .
   a. she was a good cook.
   b. he was handsome.
   c. they liked the same things.
   d. people gave them money.

PATRICK HENRY

"Give me liberty or give me death!" These famous words were spoken by Patrick Henry. His words and life changed America.

Patrick was born on May 29, 1736. He went to school at home. His father, John Henry, was his teacher. Patrick studied math, reading, and writing. He wanted to learn about the laws of the land. He studied on his own. In 1760, he took a test to become a lawyer.

At that time, the Colonies argued with the British. The British wanted to make the laws for the Colonies. They wanted Colonists to pay <u>senseless</u> taxes. In 1777, they went to war.

Patrick Henry believed that the Colonies should be free from British rules and ideas. He made a famous speech for freedom. He asked his friends to fight with him against Britain. Patrick Henry put his life on the line. He spoke those famous words, "Give me liberty or give me death!"

We must be thankful for Patrick's brave words. Most importantly, we should be thankful for his brave actions.

STORY QUESTIONS

1. Who said, "Give me liberty or give me death!"?
   a. John Henry
   b. The Colonies
   c. Patrick Henry
   d. The British

2. An **antonym** for the word *senseless* would most likely be . . .
   a. pointless.   c. silly.
   b. ridiculous.   d. practical.

3. Patrick Henry believed in freedom so much, he was willing to give his . . .
   a. family for it.   c. life for it.
   b. horse for it.   d. home for it.

4. Why did the Colonists want to be free from British rule?
   a. They were upset about the taxes, lies, and broken promises.
   b. They were upset about bad tea, angry fights, and mean words.
   c. They were upset about oceans, clothes, and guns.
   d. They were upset about animals, weapons, and fighting.

DAILY Warm-Up 18

Name _____ Date _____

BETSY ROSS

Seamstress. Designer. Businesswoman. Mother of seven. Quaker. How are these words all alike? They all describe Betsy Ross.

It is said that Betsy made the first flag, but we may never know for sure. We know that she sat on the bench in church with George Washington. She sewed buttons on his coats. She was the niece of George Ross, one of the men who signed the Declaration of Independence. Betsy also had a large sewing business in her town.

Betsy changed the original design of the flag. She made a better size and shape for the stars. She felt the stars should be in a circle. Each one should have five points, not six. The first flag had 13 stars in a circle for the 13 Colonies. Today there are 50 states and fifty stars. The colors and meaning of the flag have stayed the same. It is our symbol to the world. When people see our flag, they think of America. Hopefully, many people also think of the famous American who made it.

STORY QUESTIONS

1. What changes did Betsy make before sewing the flag?
   a. size, shape, and colors
   b. color and shape
   c. shape of the stars
   d. meaning, stitches, and the name of the flag

2. *Seamstress* most likely means . . .
   a. nibble on seams.
   b. design stars.
   c. fly flags.
   d. make dresses.

3. Which statement is **NOT** written about Betsy Ross?
   a. She had seven children.
   b. She was a mean, nasty woman.
   c. She sewed buttons onto George Washington's coats.
   d. She was a designer.

4. According to the passage, the American flag is our . . .
   a. color.   c. symbol.
   b. bird.   d. signal.

Name _____ Date _____

GHOST TOWN

An old town hides in the mountains of Montana. The name of it is Garnet. Most people today simply call it a ghost town. Many buildings still stand, but the town is silent. The last person who lived in the town of Garnet was a storeowner who died in 1947.

Garnet was started by families who came looking for gold in 1898. Over 1,000 people made their homes in the town. The men and women built the town by hand. Men worked hard inside the <u>mines</u>. They used simple hand tools and steam engines. Sixty thousand ounces of gold were mined near Garnet. Fifty thousand ounces of silver were found. Sixty thousand ounces of copper were put into mining cars.

The town was not built to last very long. After five years, the gold was almost gone. The copper was gone. Only a little silver remained. One hundred fifty people lived in the town at that point.

World War I took the men away from the town. People packed their bags. They took their families and moved away. A fire ruined most of the buildings in Garnet in 1912.

Garnet became a ghost town overnight. Today, the town of Garnet is full of history. It is a quiet place to walk around and hear whispers about life in the past.

STORY QUESTIONS

1. A *mine* is a word for . . .
   a. something that belongs to me.
   b. ghost town.
   c. an underground area that is created to get minerals.
   d. silver and gold.

2. Garnet is now . . .
   a. a river town.
   b. a seaport town.
   c. a mining town.
   d. a ghost town.

3. Why did the city of Garnet die so suddenly?
   a. The gold ran out.
   b. The silver ran out.
   c. The men went to fight in World War I.
   d. All of the above

4. A ghost town is a place . . .
   a. where there are ghost festivals each year.
   b. where you go for Halloween.
   c. that is haunted.
   d. that has been deserted—the people have all moved away.

PONY EXPRESS

When people moved west in covered wagons, things came slowly. Letters and news took a long time to get from one side of the country to the other. People had to wait for months to hear news from other places. Sometimes the mail took as long as one year, and other times it didn't arrive at all.

The Pony Express was established in 1860 to help mail and news move quickly from one place to another. Riders brought mail and messages to people who were willing to pay for it. The Pony Express gave the riders $100 dollars each month.

Each rider had to weigh less than 125 pounds. They rode in rain or snow, day or night. They often rode in very dangerous conditions. Mail carriers had to ride very fast. They would change horses every 10–15 miles at a relay station. After 100 miles, a new rider would take over.

The Pony Express did not last long because it had many problems. The people who gave money to get it started did not get much money back. The letters cost too much to send. In 1862, the Pony Express ended.

STORY QUESTIONS

1. The Pony Express was . . .
   a. a place to keep ponies.
   b. a group of horses and riders that carried mail and news across the U.S.
   c. a line of horses that had many names.
   d. a train named after a pony.

2. Which of the following could be dangers that a Pony Express rider probably faced?
   a. friendly pioneers
   b. calm streams and beautiful scenery
   c. wolves and Native American attacks
   d. wagon trains and campfires

3. If you wanted to be a rider for the Pony Express, how much could you weigh?
   a. less than 125 pounds   c. 155 pounds
   b. more than 125 pounds   d. weight didn't matter

4. According to the passage, why was the Pony Express started?
   a. so riders could get practice riding across the country
   b. to teach pioneers how to ride faster
   c. so riders could exercise their ponies
   d. to move messages and information quickly from place to place

RAILROADS

Did you know that the idea for trains started in Germany? In 1550, some roads in Germany had wooden rails. They ran along the road. They were called "<u>wagon ways</u>." These roads were used for wagons <u>pulled</u> by horses. They were easier than traveling on dirt roads.

1n 1776, metal rails were made. The rails were made of iron. They were called "tramways." They were very popular. They went all over Europe. A man named William Jesse had an idea. He made wheels with a groove, or cutout edge. These wheels helped the wagons move faster on the iron rails. The wagons were still pulled by horses.

The steam engine came next. A man named Richard Trevithick wanted to move people and things from place to place without using animals. He made the first steam engine. It could carry 10 tons of iron, 70 men, and five wagons for 9 miles in two hours.

A man named John Stevens put all of these ideas together. He is called the "father of the American railroad." He showed how steam trains would work. He got the first charter railroad.

Each new idea has made traveling easier and faster.

STORY QUESTIONS

1. Who was called the "father of the American railroad"?
   a. Richard Trevithick
   b. William Jesse
   c. Orlando Bloom
   d. John Stevens

2. Which words best describes the "wagon ways"?
   a. wooden rails
   b. iron rails
   c. steam engines
   d. fire wagons

3. Which word is an **antonym** for the word *pulled?*
   a. snatched   c. pushed
   b. grabbed   d. yanked

4. Which statement is **NOT** true about the history of the railroads?
   a. The idea for trains began in Germany.
   b. Today trains run very slowly and are pulled by horses.
   c. "Tramways" had rails made of iron.
   d. Today trains run much faster and easier than in the past.

Name _____ Date _____

TRADING POSTS ON THE OREGON TRAIL

Have you ever wondered how the pioneers lived without grocery stores? Trading posts helped families survive. Forts were built along the Oregon Trail. Each fort had a trading post. It was like a grocery store and department store put together.

The trading post was a place for the <u>weary</u> travelers to stop and rest. Trading posts stocked things the settlers needed. It was also a place to meet new people and hear any news.

The pioneers could buy rifles and bullets at the trading post. Food, such as dried meat, beans, eggs, and coffee could be bought at a trading post.

To travel safely, wagons were kept in good repair. Wagon parts, wood, hammers, saws, ropes, and chains were sold at the trading post.

Prices at the trading posts were high. Pioneers were willing to pay for things they needed. Without trading posts, many travelers would never have made it to the end of the trail.

STORY QUESTIONS

1. In the passage, *weary* means . . .
   a. excited, joyful, and nervous.
   b. happy, joyful, and angry.
   c. worn out, fatigued, and tired.
   d. mad, upset, and furious.

2. The main idea of the last paragraph is . . .
   a. to show the importance of trading posts for survival on the Oregon Trail.
   b. to show what food items a pioneer could purchase.
   c. to discuss needed equipment for a wagon.
   d. to give a list of things that people didn't want to buy at trading posts.

3. This passage was written to . . .
   a. entertain the reader with events which occurred at a trading post.
   b. inform the reader about the prices of items at the trading posts.
   c. persuade the reader to buy from a trading post.
   d. give the reader some information about trading posts.

4. According to this article, the travelers of the Oregon trail were called . . .
   a. kings.
   b. pioneers.
   c. hunters.
   d. outlaws.

DAILY Warm-Up 5

Name _____ **Date** _____

COLONIAL TOOLS AND WEAPONS

Life in Colonial times could be very difficult. The right weapons or tools for a job made it a little easier.

A sickle is a tool with a sharp blade. It has a short, wooden handle. It was used to cut grass or grain. Sickles were very helpful when clearing tall grasses for a new home or garden.

An <u>ax</u>, or axe, is another useful tool. Colonial axes had long wooden handles. The top of each axe was made out of hard silver. It could be used for chopping wood. If you wanted to build a cabin, you needed an axe.

Pistols and rifles were just as important as the other tools. They were used to protect the families from wild animals and bandits. Rifles were also used for hunting. They had long, wooden barrels. They were very heavy.

Tools and weapons were important for getting food, staying safe, and making life easier. Life depended on good tools.

STORY QUESTIONS

1. Which tool was used for cutting grasses and wheat?

a. rifle

b. axe

c. sickle

d. pistol

2. If you wanted to hunt animals, you would use . . .

a. a rifle.

b. an axe.

c. a rope.

d. a sickle.

3. The author's purpose for this passage is to . . .

a. entertain the reader with funny information about tools.

b. inform the reader about the job of the axe.

c. show the importance of tools and weapons to the Colonial families.

d. teach the reader how to use a sickle.

4. Another name for an *ax* is . . .

a. a wagon.

c. a sickle.

b. an axe.

d. a horse.

Name _____   Date _____

COLONIAL ANIMALS

In Colonial times, people used animals for many things. Horses moved people from place to place. Plowing the fields was done by oxen because they were strong. Cows and goats gave milk for butter and cheese. Chickens provided eggs and meat. Bees made honey that Colonists used to sweeten food and drinks. They also made beeswax that could be used for candles.

Many Colonists built outside stalls to house their larger animals, such as horses and cows. Others built barns with pens inside them. Chickens were put inside <u>coops</u> made of wire and wood, with a door at one end. Pigsties were built for the pigs. These were wooden pens with large flat places for them to sleep or lie down.

Beehives were made out of wood or straw. These hives were put in gardens so that the bees could collect pollen from flowers and make honey.

Taking care of the animals was needed to take care of one's own family.

STORY QUESTIONS

1. Why did the Colonists care for their livestock?
a. so the animals would enjoy summer vacation
b. so the animals would grow very large
c. so the animals would provide food and transportation for them
d. so the animals would have a nice place to live

2. A *coop* is a type of . . .
a. shelter for birds.
b. hole in the ground.
c. rock in a garden.
d. wagon on a farm.

3. If your family owned a horse in Colonial times, you would most likely use it for . . .
a. hanging your clothes on.
b. getting from one place to another.
c. making milk for butter and cheese.
d. racing.

4. Most enclosures for the animals were made of . . .
a. mud.   c. silver.
b. gold.   d. wood.

DAILY
Warm-Up 7

Name _____ Date _____

THE WILDERNESS

The Pilgrims came to the New World to find a new life. They did not know how hard it would be. They did not know they would live in such <u>wilderness</u>.

The land needed clearing. Rocks and tree stumps were pulled from the ground. Logs from the trees were used to make homes and furniture. Scraps became firewood. Crops had to be planted and barns had to built.

The Pilgrims had to build the barns before they built their own homes. Otherwise the animals wouldn't survive the long winter. The first homes were little more than holes dug in the ground. The dirt was cold and damp, and the fires filled the homes with smoke.

Eventually, the Pilgrims made houses out of wood. They used axes to chop trees and strip bark off the logs. They cut notches in the wood to help lock the logs together. Each house was just one room in which the whole family cooked, ate, and slept. The homes all had a fireplace in the room that was used for heat and light. There was no electricity.

When the Pilgrims came to America, they faced challenges they had never imagined.

STORY QUESTIONS

1. *Wilderness* probably means . . .
   a. a park with animals.
   b. a place in a big city.
   c. a zoo.
   d. a place not yet touched by humans.

2. Which tool was most helpful when building cabins?
   a. an axe
   b. a rifle
   c. a sickle
   d. a petticoat

3. In the passage above, the fireplace was used for . . .
   a. water and heat.
   b. heat and light.
   c. a place to cook and make candles.
   d. cooking and cleaning.

4. The second paragraph is mainly about . . .
   a. the importance of the fireplace.
   b. what the Pilgrims had to do to create a place to live.
   c. planting crops and baking bread.
   d. a trip to Alaska.

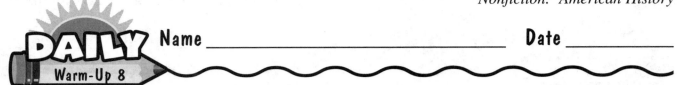

Name _____   Date _____

COLONIAL GARDENS

Do you like to garden? It's fun to watch plants and flowers grow. Family gardens were once necessary. In the early Colonial days, every family grew their own food.

Wealthy families grew large gardens. They needed many workers. Some had fancy gardens with paths down the middle. Some formed shapes of squares, diamonds, and circles. These Colonists paid gardeners to cut the shrubs and bushes. In warm weather, they invited friends over to sit in their gardens. The gardens were beautiful and peaceful.

Most families tended their own gardens. The gardens were used to grow food to feed the family. Apple and peach trees were grown for fruit. Cabbage, turnips, carrots, pumpkins, and beans were vegetables they grew.

Herbs were grown in the gardens to be used for medicine. Herbs could also be added to food to give it a better flavor.

Extra fruits and vegetables were grown in the summer. The extras were then saved and dried. They were stored for the winter months when fruits and vegetables were scarce.

STORY QUESTIONS

1. How did Colonists feed their families fruits and vegetables?
   a. They bought them at the market.
   b. They ordered their groceries online.
   c. They bought them from friends.
   d. They raised all their own fruits and vegetables.

2. Why did the Colonists grow extra fruits and vegetables in the summer?
   a. They had to save them for the winter months.
   b. They had to save them for a big party at the end of the summer.
   c. They liked to make pies with all the extra fruit.
   d. None of the above.

3. The author's purpose for this passage is . . .
   a. to provide information on Colonial gardens.
   b. to persuade the reader to eat vegetables.
   c. to entertain the reader with veggie jokes.
   d. none of the above.

4. How were the gardens of the wealthy different from those who were not wealthy?
   a. They weren't different. They were all the same.
   b. They were bigger, and they had other people help with gardening.
   c. Wealthy people's gardens were green. The other gardens were brown.
   d. All of the above.

Name _____   Date _____

DIARIES

Did you know that diaries are historical documents? Diaries from the past tell stories of days gone by. The people who wrote them took the time to write things as they saw them. They give details about events and people they knew. Each writer comes alive in the words they wrote on the paper. Diaries help us to learn about how people lived and what was important to them.

Diaries of the pioneers on the Oregon Trail help us to understand the hard times those people faced. They tell how they came looking for land to build homes. Diaries tell stories about traveling in covered wagons. They describe how children walked alongside the wagons and often wore no shoes on the path. They tell of snakes and wild animals and crossing wild river waters. Diaries describe attacks, how many travelers got sick, and how it felt to reach their goals.

Many diaries of the Oregon Trail have been made into books. These diaries, or records, help us understand how people lived on the Oregon Trail. They help us understand what went right and what went wrong. These diaries help us learn from their mistakes. They show us how to enjoy the simple things in life.

STORY QUESTIONS

1. What are some of the hardships listed above that pioneers had to face?
   a. sickness, snow, and no electricity
   b. ants, wasps, and other poisonous bugs
   c. sickness, snakes, and attacks
   d. no water

2. Which of the following diary entries was most likely written by a pioneer?
   a. One of the wheels broke on the wagon today.
   b. Lots of traffic on the freeway today.
   c. Finished making our cement house today.
   d. Bought the kids their first computer today.

3. In this passage, the author states that diaries from the past are helpful us because . . .
   a. they are pretty to look at.
   b. they tell us how the writer felt and what he or she saw and heard.
   c. they show us handwriting from the past.
   d. none of the above.

4. If there were no diaries of the past, we would . . .
   a. have too much information.
   b. not have any information about Mount Everest.
   c. not know much of what happened in past time periods.
   d. not understand how to play board games.

DAILY Warm-Up 10

Name _____ Date _____

RACING TO THE GOLD

"There's gold in them thar hills!" James Marshall started a gold rush when he found the first piece of gold in California in 1849. People raced to northern California, hoping to make their fortune.

There were many ways to get to the gold sites. Miners traveled over land on foot or with a team of oxen. This trip could take as long four months. The trail was long and dusty.

Travelers could sail on the ocean. It could take from four months to a year to arrive. Sailing cost a lot of money. Many sailing travelers never got to the mining sites at all.

Another way to travel was by air. A new machine that looked like a balloon flew miners to California. More than 200 people wanted to take a ride in the balloon. They paid money and signed up for the trip, but the balloons never got off the ground.

Wind wagons were another way some miners used to travel. A wind wagon looked like a wagon, but it had sails like a ship. It moved faster than a wagon by using the wind to move it along. However, they were dangerous and hard to drive. Many miners did not know how to steer it, so they often crashed.

Would-be miners made great efforts to cash in on the gold craze. Some were big winners. Others never found gold.

The San Francisco professional football team, the 49ers, is a tribute to the spirit of the brave people who took a chance.

STORY QUESTIONS

1. When did the great gold rush of California begin?
   a. 1776
   b. 1849
   c. 1944
   d. None of the above.

2. Another title for this passage could be . . .
   a. "Miners of the Gold Rush."
   b. "Mines of California."
   c. "Getting to the Gold Rush."
   d. "Leaving the Gold Rush."

3. The balloons could never reach California because . . .
   a. they couldn't get them to fly in the air.
   b. they cost too much.
   c. they were ugly.
   d. All of the above.

4. The San Francisco 49ers are a . . .
   a. basketball team.
   b. sewing group.
   c. boy band.
   d. football team.

GOLD COUNTRY '49

Most people who came to California in 1849 were looking for gold. Some men came to make money in other ways.

In 1853, a man made a pair of pants on an old sewing machine. The pants were made out of canvas. They were strong and long lasting. In just a few months, his pants became popular with miners. He could hardly sew pants fast enough to keep up with the number of people that wanted to buy them. He got rich overnight. What was his name? Levi Strauss. He made the first pair of Levi's jeans.

Phillip Armour lived in New York. He decided he would walk to California. He stopped in a town called Placerville, California. He opened a store and sold meat. Phillip made so much money that he moved his meat plant to Wisconsin. He became the largest meat maker in the world. He made Armour hot dogs and sausages.

Henry Wells and William Fargo moved to San Francisco. They had a stagecoach company and started a bank. Mail was moved from place to place on their stagecoaches. People put money in their bank. Henry and William kept it safe. They let others who needed money use it, if they paid it back. Wells Fargo was the name of their company. Today, it does not carry mail. It does not bring people on a stagecoach. It is a bank that is found in towns across the United States. The name is still Wells Fargo.

These men did not find gold in pans. They did not look for it in the streams. They got their money from their new ideas.

STORY QUESTIONS

1. Which man is responsible for Levi jeans?
a. Henry Wells
b. Levi Strauss
c. William Fargo
d. Phillip Armour

2. Which of the following statements is **FALSE**?
a. Levi Strauss helped create Wells Fargo bank.
b. Many people came to California for reasons other than gold.
c. Gold mining was not the only industry in California.
d. The men mentioned above did not pan for gold. They made their money creating other things.

3. The purpose of this passage is to . . .
a. entertain the reader with stories and diaries of miners.
b. inform the reader about the steps of panning for gold.
c. persuade the reader to learn more about California missions.
d. to inform the reader about other ways people made money in California.

4. Which of the following was **NOT** one of the ways of making money mentioned in the passage above?
a. making pants
b. selling meat
c. baking bread
d. bringing mail by stagecoach

Name _____ Date _____

CIVIL WAR WEAPONS

What weapons were used during the Civil War? The <u>revolver</u> was made especially for the war. This gun would shoot easily. It was strong and long lasting. The man who made the revolver sold 12,000 of these guns to the government for the soldiers. The soldiers in the North used these guns. These guns were so well built that some people smuggled them to the soldiers in the South.

Rifles were also very important in the war. They were made out of wood and metal. Most of them were very heavy. They had a wooden handle and long barrels. Most rifles used gunpowder.

There were at least 12 different types of rifles to buy. The most useful was the rifle that was copied from the British. It was called a musket. It could shoot up to 1,100 feet and hit most of the targets. It only weighed 9 pounds and 3 ounces. Most rifles were much heavier. They also came with a knife on the end of the gun called a bayonet. This was very helpful when the soldiers were fighting by hand.

The revolver and the rifle were the most useful weapons of the Civil War.

STORY QUESTIONS

1. What does the passage mention about the rifle that was copied from the British?
   a. It could shoot quite far, had a bayonet on it, and only weighed about 9 pounds.
   b. It was very nice looking.
   c. It was long, thin, and shot bullets.
   d. It was made by Benjamin Franklin.

2. Which sentence best describes a revolver in the passage?
   a. It shoots 1,000 feet and weighs 20 pounds.
   b. It fires a small bullet.
   c. It is strong, long lasting, and shoots easily.
   d. It was not useful in the Civil War.

3. Which of the following is a **synonym** for *revolver*?
   a. cannon
   b. rifle
   c. bomb
   d. handgun

4. Which statement is **TRUE** from the passage above?
   a. Most weapons were not useful in the Civil War.
   b. The rifle copied after the British rifle had a bayonet.
   c. Revolvers were very heavy.
   d. Revolvers were patterned after British guns.

DAILY Name _____ Date _____
Warm-Up 13

MAP SKILLS

Have you ever used a map to find your way to a special place? Maps show directions, but maps have other jobs, too. If you want to learn about the world, study maps.

Regional maps show us where different groups of people can be found. They show us where different tribes lived in the United States. They show us information about the weather in areas. They can show us where to find different religions of the world.

Product maps show us the kinds of things that farmers grow. They show us the animals that the farmers raise. This kind of map shows us that farmers in Iowa grow corn and wheat. It shows us that the farmers in Texas raise cattle.

Density maps compare numbers of people living in one place to numbers of people living elsewhere.

Route maps show the path or movement of a group of people. We can use a route map to find out where Christopher Columbus sailed his ships. They can show us the way that supplies are moved across an area. They can show us where the pioneers went across the trails.

Each kind of map gives different information. Think about what you are looking for. What do you want to learn? Find the map that is best and dig in!

STORY QUESTIONS

1. If you wanted to find out what states the Oregon Trail went through, you would probably use a . . .
   a. product map.   c. density map.
   b. regional map.   d. route map.

2. What were some of the products listed that could be found on product maps?
   a. cattle, corn, and wheat
   b. corn, strawberries, and hay
   c. cattle, sheep, and horses
   d. corn, wheat, and lettuce

3. What kind of map would tell you about rainfall in an area?
   a. a regional map   c. a density map
   b. a product map   d. a route map

4. Which statement is **TRUE** from the passage above?
   a. Regional maps compare movements of goods.
   b. Density maps compare populations in different areas of the country or world.
   c. Product maps show number of people in certain areas.
   d. Route maps show what animals farmers raise and crops they grow.

Name _____   Date _____

DECLARATION OF INDEPENDENCE

On July 4, 1776, the Declaration of Independence of the United States of America was signed. Fifty-six men put their names on the document. This act showed that the Colonies would not follow the <u>rules</u> of the English any more. This act changed the course of history.

These men did not agree with the rules of England. The Declaration listed 18 ways that the British had done a bad job. These men wrote clearly that the English did not pay attention to the things they needed. The English did not care about their feelings. They did not care about their wishes.

As a result, they wrote this declaration to say that they were going to be free from England. They felt it was important to have full power to make contracts with whomever they wanted. They wanted power to trade with whomever they chose, whenever they wanted to trade.

Lastly, they wanted full power to decide their future. These men wanted to make the choices that were best for themselves and the people who lived in the Colonies.

On July 4, 1776, all 56 men signed the declaration. They promised to give their lives for each other. They promised to share what they had with each other. They promised to respect each other.

These men wanted to be free. Free to choose. Free to speak. Free to live in the way they thought was best.

STORY QUESTIONS

1. What is another word for *rules* in this passage?
   a. freedom
   b. a piece of paper
   c. laws
   d. choices

2. Which words best describe the Colonists?
   a. had their minds made up to give their lives to make things better in the Colonies
   b. happy with the way things were
   c. sad because they did not have all the conveniences of the British
   d. angry because they could not build cabins and cities fast enough

3. What is one thing listed in the passage the Colonists wanted to change?
   a. They wanted to choose with whom they would play.
   b. They wanted to choose with whom they would trade.
   c. They wanted to choose what language to speak.
   d. They wanted to choose what food to eat.

4. Which statement is **TRUE** from the passage above?
   a. The Colonists agreed with British laws.
   b. The Colonists wanted to move back to England.
   c. The Colonists wanted to use laws from France.
   d. The Colonists wanted to make their own laws.

Name _____ Date _____

JAMESTOWN

Three ships left England in December of 1606. There were more than one hundred passengers on the ships. Most were upper class Englishmen. There were no women at all.

They came to the coast of Virginia in April of 1607. They wanted to find a good place to anchor the ship. They looked for a place that would be safe for them to live.

On May 14, 1607, they landed on Jamestown Island. The water was deep so they could get close to shore. They were sure the ship would be safe in the trees.

There were problems in Jamestown from the start. One group of Native Americans attacked the settlers shortly after they landed. There was <u>disease</u>. There was not enough food. Many settlers starved to death. There were more Native American attacks.

John Rolfe finally brought a few years of peace to Jamestown. He came to grow tobacco. He married Pocahontas, the daughter of a Native American Chief. The peace with the Native Americans did not last forever, but it was a start.

STORY QUESTIONS

1. According to the passage, what was the first problem the settlers faced in Jamestown?
   a. bad weather
   b. starvation
   c. disease
   d. Native American attacks

2. About long did it take to get to Jamestown Island?
   a. 5 months
   b. 11 months
   c. 10 months
   d. 3 months

3. A **synonym** for the word *disease* would be . . .
   a. Christmas.
   b. birthday.
   c. sickness.
   d. health.

4. What did John Rolfe grow when he came to Jamestown?
   a. corn
   b. tobacco
   c. cigarettes
   d. wheat

COLONIAL WILLIAMSBURG

The town of Jamestown collapsed. It was swampy. It had insects. The settlers were starving. Many Native American tribes had attacked.

Settlers wanted to move to a better place. They looked for higher ground. They wanted to be closer to the James and York Rivers. They like the idea of being safer from attacks.

Middle Plantation was the answer. By 1609, the settlers built a small town. It was safer and on higher ground. It was close to both rivers. Some of the settlers planned out the town using patterns of squares. As the town grew, people built stores and mills. There were churches and homes, and even taverns.

The people wanted to give the town a new name. They wanted it to be in honor of William II, the King of England. They named it Williamsburg.

By the time of the Revolutionary War, the city had 2,000 people. There were tailors, carpenters, and bakers. There were gunsmiths and store clerks. The small town had turned into a bustling city.

STORY QUESTIONS

1. What was one of the reasons that settlers wanted to move away from Jamestown?
   a. They wanted to be closer to England.
   b. They wanted to be closer to New York.
   c. They wanted to be closer to the York River.
   d. They wanted to be closer to the Native Americans.

2. If you lived in Williamsburg, you might have a job as . . .
   a. an airline pilot.   c. a TV repair person.
   b. a tailor.   d. a taxi driver.

3. Which is **NOT** something you would find in Williamsburg?
   a. a gunsmith
   b. a bakery
   c. a fast food restaurant
   d. churches

4. Why did the settlers change the name from Middle Plantation to Williamsburg?
   a. They liked how it sounded.
   b. They named it after the king of England.
   c. They were bored of the old name.
   d. They did it to make people jealous.

DAILY
Warm-Up 17

Name _____ Date _____

COMMUNITIES LONG AGO

Long ago it was hard to get news from place to place. Traveling took a lot of time. Most people had to walk. Some rode horses or buggies; others traveled in boats. People called town criers walked through town yelling the news. Few towns had newspapers.

In 1807, Robert Fulton invented the steamboat. It was a boat that moved up and down the river using steam. It was the first boat to move without paddles.

In 1844, the telegraph machine was invented by Samuel Morse. This new tool brought people together. It could send messages over electric wires. The machine used a special code to send messages. Cities and towns far apart could share the news in minutes.

In 1860, the Pony Express took mail across the United States. Riders were paid to carry mail in leather bags. New riders took the bags every 80 to 100 miles. They got fresh horses every 10 to 15 miles so the could keep the horses from getting too tired.

In 1908, the first plane was invented. Wilber and Orville Wright flew the first plane.

STORY QUESTIONS

1. Robert Fulton's new boat was powered by . . .
   a. steam.
   b. gasoline.
   c. horses.
   d. manpower.

2. Which word or words best describe Samuel Morse, Orville and Wilber Wright, and Robert Fulton?
   a. police officers
   b. criminals
   c. inventors
   d. riders

3. Which words in the passage mean the same as the word *exhausted?*
   a. place to place
   b. wait a long time
   c. full of energy
   d. too tired

4. If you wanted to send a message in the year 1846, what was the fastest way to send it?
   a. Pony Express
   b. telegraph
   c. US Postal Service
   d. UPS

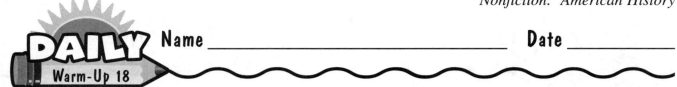

Name _____   Date _____

COMMUNITIES TODAY

Life in the present day has changed from years ago. Today everything is <u>instant</u>. Cars are fast. Food is fast. Technology is fast.

Traveling is also different today from years ago. Cars, buses, trucks, or vans move us quickly where we want to go. People travel by subways. Subways are trains that run mostly under the ground. Other people travel in planes. They can move us from one part of the world to another in only one day. Astronauts travel to the moon in space shuttles. Shuttles travel faster than planes or cars.

Communication has become very fast as well. People can use cell phones and computers to deliver messages instantly. Televisions and radios broadcast the news that is happening right now. We no longer have to wait months to receive information from other parts of the world.

STORY QUESTIONS

1. What would be one word or group of words that describes communities today?
   a. backwards, quick
   b. old fashioned, slow
   c. advanced, fast
   d. out of date

2. Which would be a **synonym** for *instant?*
   a. quick
   b. slow
   c. immediate
   d. fast

3. Which sentence below makes the most sense?
   a. Communication today is much slower than in years past.
   b. Communication today is much faster than in years past.
   c. Today's communities are no different from communities years ago.
   d. Today's communities are very similar to communities years ago.

4. Which statement is **NOT** mentioned in the passage above?
   a. Transportation can be in a car, van, plane, or train.
   b. Space shuttles travel faster than cars or planes.
   c. Wagons are the most common form of transportation in 2006.
   d. Communication can take place on a computer or on a cell phone.

DAILY
Warm-Up 1

Name _____ Date _____

CLASSIFYING ANIMALS

Did you know that there are over 1,000,000 different species, or types, of animals? With so many species, scientists have to find a way to sort them into groups. Two of the main groups are vertebrates and invertebrates.

Vertebrates are animals that have a backbone. Humans are in this group. Also in this group are whales, monkeys, birds, and frogs. Just about any pet you have in your home is a vertebrate. Dogs, cats, goldfish, hamsters, and snakes are vertebrates.

Invertebrates have no backbone. Many of them live in the ocean. Clams, jellyfish, squids, and octopuses are invertebrates. Those that live on land are spiders, worms, and insects.

Scientists are finding new species of animals every day. Every one of them can be put into one of these two groups.

STORY QUESTIONS

1. What are two ways, according to this passage, animals are classified or sorted?
   a. land and water animals
   b. mammals and jellyfish
   c. invertebrates and vertebrates
   d. color and shape

2. Based on the passage, which is the best definition of invertebrates?
   a. animals that have several backbones
   b. animals that have one backbone
   c. animals that have no backbones
   d. animals that prefer to swim in the ocean

3. Human beings are in the category of . . .
   a. invertebrates.
   b. vertebrates.
   c. neither of these.
   d. both of these.

4. Which of the animals below would fit into the category of invertebrates?
   a. giraffe
   b. bird
   c. squid
   d. pig

PLANTS

It is important for scientists to sort animals into groups. It just as important to sort plants. Scientists sort them by how they make another plant like themselves. This is called <u>reproduction</u>. Scientists have decided to sort plants into three groups.

The first group of plants reproduces with spores. Spores are parts of the plant that break away and travel in the wind. Each one grows into a new plant if it lands on soil that is wet and rich. Ferns and mosses are plants that make a copy of themselves with spores.

Other plants reproduce with seeds. They are the second group. Seeds fall from the trees. They become part of the soil and grow into new plants. Evergreens, pine trees, and fir trees are plants that reproduce with seeds.

The third group is the plant that reproduces by flowering. Before seeds can form, the pollen inside the flower needs to move from one part of the flower to another. The seeds form inside the flower. Birds and insects help this by moving the pollen when they land on the flower. Some of the flowering plants grow into fruits to eat. The seeds are hidden inside the fruit. Apples, oranges, cherries, daisies, and roses are plants that have flowers.

STORY QUESTIONS

1. Which group of words mean the same as the word *reproduction*?
a. make a copy of itself   c. plants the flowers
b. helps us understand   d. flowering and pollen

2. Scientists have broken plants into three different groups:
a. colors, sizes, and shapes.
b. spores, flowers, and seeds.
c. vertebrates, invertebrates, and seeds.
d. cherries, grapes, and oranges.

3. How do the plants that have spores reproduce?
a. by seeds falling on the ground
b. by floating in the wind from place to place
c. by bees moving the pollen inside the flowers
d. by pushing their roots into the ground

4. Which type of plant group needs help from birds or insects?
a. plants that reproduce with spores
b. plants that reproduce with flowers
c. plants that reproduce with leaves
d. plants that reproduce with sunlight

Name _____ Date _____

FORESTS

Forests can be found all around the world. There are many different plants and animals that use the forest as their home.

In the forest, small animals eat the fruits, nuts, mushrooms, and insects. They race around from tree to tree and jump from branch to branch. Larger animals eat smaller animals. Other animals eat seeds and <u>shrubs</u>. Even though most animals are scared of humans, they are never far away. An ant, bat, robin, snake, deer, or turkey may be hiding among the leaves. They may be sitting in the trees. They might be running on the ground.

Many different types of trees live in the forest. Trees drop their leaves during the fall to save water on the floor of the forest. The soil is made up of fallen leaves, dirt, and animals that have died. After the animals and plants die, their bodies break down. This makes the earth rich with nutrients.

Forests are fun places to visit. A person who wants to see and hear the real sounds of the forest must sit quietly and listen with his or her eyes and ears.

STORY QUESTIONS

1. Which type of area is the article describing?

   a. mountains   c. desert

   b. ocean   d. forest

2. If you were to close your eyes in the forest, which one of these sounds might you hear?

   a. a squirrel chattering with its friend

   b. breaking glass

   c. waves crashing on the rocks

   d. sea gulls screeching

3. The purpose of this passage is . . .

   a. to entertain the reader with forest crafts he or she can make.

   b. to inform the reader of interesting facts about a forest.

   c. to persuade the reader to travel to a forest on vacation.

   d. to encourage the reader to create his or her own forest.

4. A good **synonym** for the word *shrub* could be . . .

   a. dog.

   b. bush.

   c. bird.

   d. sand.

OCEANS

Are you looking for some place new to explore? The ocean is an amazing part of our earth. There are many parts to the ocean and many different types of animals that live in it.

Coral reefs give food and shelter to small animals that live near the top of the water. Coral reefs are warm and usually have plenty of light. Starfish, sea anemones, and clams live here.

The seashore is the part of the ocean most of us know best. It includes the sand but also tide pools along the rocks. Animals that live on the rocks have special arms and legs that help them when the waves crash over them. They use these arms and legs to hold onto the rocks around them. Other animals, like crabs and some birds, move every time the waves crash back and forth. Smaller animals stay alive by quickly digging holes into the sand.

Many sea animals live in the open ocean where the waters still have some light. Many types of plants, as well as sharks, fish, turtles, and seals live here.

Deep down in the ocean it is very cold. There is very little light. In the deepest parts of the ocean, it is completely dark. Some animals that live down there actually create their own light to attract other fish!

STORY QUESTIONS

1. Why would you probably not find a coral reef in the deep ocean?
   a. Reefs need cold water to live.
   b. Reefs need light and warm water to live.
   c. Reefs need to live in dark parts of the ocean.
   d. Reefs wouldn't have enough food in the deep.

2. How do some of the smaller sand animals survive on the seashore?
   a. They grab onto the coral reef.
   b. They roll with the waves.
   c. They hold on to rocks.
   d. They tunnel quickly down into the sand.

3. According to the passage, what can some animals that live in the deep ocean do?
   a. They can go for long periods of time without eating.
   b. They can create their own light.
   c. They can swim with their eyes closed.
   d. They can eat animals larger than themselves.

4. If you were to explore the seashore, which of these would you probably feel beneath your toes?
   a. sand, ice, and snow
   b. ice, snow, and mud
   c. sand, small pebbles, and shells
   d. large rocks, clay, and chunks of dirt

DESERTS

It might seem that very few things can survive in the desert. Most plants and animals that you see in your town probably wouldn't. But there are many different types of plants and animals that are perfectly suited to the hot, dry climate.

In the desert, there is very little water. The plants and animals that live in the desert have special features for living with little water. Plants like the cactus have short leaves. These leaves trap and store water. The cactus also has spines on its leaves. This is to keep animals from taking its water.

Animals that live in the desert are often nocturnal. This means they sleep during the day. They come out to eat at night when it is cool. Other animals, like the camel, are awake during the heat of the day. They have special eyelashes that keep the sand out of their eyes. They have nostrils that can close to keep the sand out of their noses. They can go for many days without drinking. Many animals that live in the desert can get all the water they need from the foods they eat.

STORY QUESTIONS

1. Which of these could be a title for this passage?
   a. "A Cold Day in the Desert"
   b. "How to Stay Cool in the Desert"
   c. "Plant and Animal Life in the Desert"
   d. "When You are Hot, Drink Water"

2. What makes camels a unique or special animal?
   a. They are used to humans so they eat from our hands.
   b. They are awake at night when it's cool.
   c. They have special eyelashes and nostrils to help keep sand out of their bodies.
   d. They live under rocks.

3. Animals that sleep during the day are called . . .
   a. lazy.
   b. desert creatures.
   c. camels.
   d. nocturnal.

4. If you wanted to visit the desert in the daytime, you might wear . . .
   a. a heavy jacket, mittens, and a hat.
   b. shorts, a tank top, and sunglasses.
   c. long jeans, a sweater, and rain gear.
   d. a swimsuit and goggles.

Name _____ Date _____

TUNDRA

Do you think the desert is the only place that has very little rain? The tundra doesn't get much rain either. It is different from the desert, though. The tundra is almost always frozen!

The tundra is one of the coldest habitats on the earth. Summer only lasts for two months. During this time, the ground thaws, or melts, a little. It is never very warm, though. During the winter, there are times when the sun doesn't shine at all.

Only a few plants are able to stay alive in this habitat. When the icy winds blow, they are only safe because they grow close to the ground. Animals such as reindeer, polar bears, and musk oxen are the only ones that can stay alive in this cold weather. They have very thick fur that keeps them warm. Some of these animals hibernate in the winter while others migrate south.

The plants and animals of the tundra have adapted to this harsh environment.

STORY QUESTIONS

1. Summer in the tundra is . . .
   a. hot and dry.
   b. very busy.
   c. two months long.
   d. cold and rainy.

2. If you were to visit the tundra, you might expect to see . . .
   a. parks, benches, and swing sets.
   b. flowers, trees, and large bushes.
   c. low-lying plants and a few animals.
   d. birds, cats, and dogs.

3. A person who plans to visit the tundra should probably wear . . .
   a. shorts and sunglasses.
   b. a light jacket and a baseball cap.
   c. a heavy jacket, warm hat, and gloves.
   d. skis.

4. How are the tundra and a desert similar?
   a. They are not similar at all.
   b. They both have lots of different types of plants.
   c. They have the same types of plants and animals.
   d. They both get very little rain.

Name _____

Date _____

TROPICAL RAINFORESTS

Rainforests are very warm, wet forests. Rain falls for days and even months. Rainforests have millions of different types of plants and animals. They live in the four different zones of the rainforest.

The first <u>zone</u> is called the emergent zone. This is high above the rainforest. Here, giant trees stretch higher than the average height of any of the other plants. Many birds and insects live here.

The second zone is the canopy. This is the leafy area of the tops of the trees. Most of the animals in the rainforest live here. You can find monkeys, parrots, and frogs up here. You can also find butterflies, snakes, and sloths. A sloth is a very slow-moving animal that hangs upside down from the trees.

The understory is the third zone. It is made up of mostly young trees and shrubs. It is dark and cool. It is under the leaves, but not on the ground.

The forest floor is the final zone of the rainforest. The largest animals, such as jaguars and even elephants usually live here. The forest floor is also home to millions and millions of insects!

STORY QUESTIONS

1. In which zone would you most likely find a large animal, such as a jaguar?
   a. emergent zone
   b. canopy
   c. understory
   d. forest floor

2. According to the passage, how many types of plants and animals live in the rainforest?
   a. trillions
   b. millions
   c. kazillions
   d. thousands

3. Which is the highest zone in the rainforest?
   a. forest floor
   b. emergent
   c. canopy
   d. understory

4. In this passage, *zone* probably means . . .
   a. time zone.
   b. area under water.
   c. part or section.
   d. area where no animals live.

Name _____   Date _____

BRAIN POWER

In 2001, Matt Nagle was a 25-year-old football star. Then one night he had a bad accident that resulted in his spinal cord being cut.

Matt was paralyzed from the neck down. He could not do anything alone. Matt couldn't even breathe by himself. Doctors kept working to make better equipment for people like Matt to stay alive. Science labs kept doing research to try and find answers. They were trying to make machines to help paralyzed patients. A company who does research on brains was searching for ways to use brain waves. They chose Matt as the first person to try a new technology. They wanted to do an experiment that used machines to carry out instructions from inside the brain.

In June 2004, the doctors <u>implanted a chip into Matt's brain</u>. This chip could run machines with his thoughts. Matt could send simple messages to a computer with this chip. He could change channels on the TV. Matt could play computer games and turn lights on and off. All of these things he could do just by thinking about them.

Matt worked for months to get the messages to move from his brain to the computer. It was very hard. The technology was difficult. The doctors were worried that the chip might injure Matt's body. They also worried that it might hurt his brain and his thinking. Matt wanted to fight to get better. Matt kept fighting in hopes of trying to help make things better for other people like himself.

STORY QUESTIONS

1. "Implanted a chip into Matt's brain" means . . .
   a. planted a flower in his brain.
   b. placed a computer chip into his brain.
   c. added cookies to his brain.
   d. placed tortilla chips in his brain.

2. What did the doctors worry would happen when they put the chip into Matt's brain?
   a. There would be damage to his mind and to his body.
   b. He would get cancer.
   c. He would start singing and dancing.
   d. He would start swimming and golfing.

3. What can Matt use his mind to do?
   a. type letters, dial the phone, and play cards
   b. run, jump, and dance
   c. turn lights on and off, switch TV channels, and play computer games
   d. play football

4. From reading this passage, we can guess that Matt was a person who . . .
   a. didn't like to do hard things.   c. never gave up.
   b. was a show off.   d. yelled a lot.

DAILY
Warm-Up 9

Name _____ Date _____

SOFT T-REX

In 2005, there was an <u>unusual</u> discovery found in Montana. Twenty-four different kinds of dinosaurs were uncovered in this one place. One kind was different than all of the others. Most dinosaurs that are discovered are just bones. This dinosaur still had soft tissue. It had cells and blood vessels. This was not known when the dinosaur was first discovered. A scientist discovered it when she examined it in the lab.

Before this discovery, scientists never thought that tissue in bones could survive more than 100,000 years. The scientists tested the bones. They found that they were 68 million years old. This was the oldest dinosaur ever discovered with tissue.

This type of tissue is found in bones of birds when they are ready to make eggshells. It contains calcium. It is found when birds are ready to lay eggs. The scientists realized they had found a female dinosaur. This dinosaur had laid eggs. The eggs from this dinosaur were very much like bird eggs today.

STORY QUESTIONS

1. An **antonym** for the word *unusual* would be . . .
   a. regular.
   b. strange.
   c. odd.
   d. bizarre.

2. Why was this dinosaur so important?
   a. It had to be taken out with a helicopter.
   b. It was the biggest dinosaur ever discovered.
   c. It was the first dinosaur over 100,000 years old with soft tissue.
   d. It was in the middle of a lot of other dinosaurs.

3. What did the bone have inside?
   a. a bone that is long, thin, and yellow
   b. a bone that cannot be broken
   c. a material that has calcium inside
   d. dinosaur babies

4. Why was this discovery so important?
   a. It showed that this dinosaur laid eggs like our modern day birds.
   b. It showed that this dinosaur laid eggs like our modern day crocodiles.
   c. It showed that this dinosaur laid eggs like our modern day squirrels.
   d. It showed that dinosaurs didn't lay eggs.

DAILY Name _____ Date _____
Warm-Up 10

NEW PLANET?

On January 8, 2005, three scientists were studying the solar system. They were surprised to see something new in the sky. It was large and bright. Even people who studied the stars for fun were able to see it. These people are called <u>amateur astronomers</u>.

The object was much bigger than Pluto. Its orbit, or path, around the sun was different from the other planets. People started asking questions. Was it a planet or not? No one knew for sure. Everyone had his or her own opinion.

Michael A. Brown, one of the three scientists, believed it was a planet because of its size and distance. A man named Alan Boss did not agree. Alan is a <u>theorist</u>, a person who studies guesses. He believes that if we call it a "planet," we are not being fair to the bigger planets in the solar system.

Michael Brown has continued to collect information on the bright object. He feels sure it is a planet. He is trying to find out about how big it is. He wants to know how much it weighs. He wants to know what it is made of.

Michael has made up a name for the planet. However, he is keeping the name a secret. He won't tell until it is known if it is really a planet or just another bright light in the sky.

STORY QUESTIONS

1. What is an *amateur astronomer?*
   a. a person who likes stars, ice cream, and cookies
   b. a person who has a college degree in astronomy
   c. a person who studies the stars and the sky for fun
   d. a person who sits on his porch to catch snowflakes

2. A *theorist* is someone who . . .
   a. enjoys talking about stars.
   b. chats with friends about things they do not know.
   c. studies guesses to find out if they are true.
   d. studies the stars.

3. Why hasn't Michael told everyone the name he wishes to give the planet?
   a. It hasn't been proven yet that it is a planet.
   b. He might change the name.
   c. He is too embarrassed.
   d. He wants someone else to name it now.

4. Why were amateur scientists able to see this new object in the sky?
   a. It cut off the sun for 10 minutes.
   b. They knew it was coming.
   c. They had read science fiction novels about it.
   d. It was very bright and large.

DAILY
Warm-Up 1

Name _____ Date _____

RECYCLING

Have you ever thought about the fact that most of what you own will one day be thrown out? Think about your clothes, the TV, and the stove. They will tear or break down. Or you may just want to get new, better things. But where do things go when you throw them out?

The bad news is that most of it goes to a landfill. A landfill is a big hole in the ground. It may have a concrete or plastic liner. This liner keeps chemicals from seeping into the groundwater around the landfill. Trash trucks filled with all the things that people throw out go to the landfill. They dump their loads into the hole. Bulldozers cover everything with soil. But there is a better way. And since we are running out of landfill space, more people are doing it.

The better way is recycling. Recycling lets many things be used again. Give away an old TV or stove. They can be fixed so that someone else can use them. Clothes can be sent to people who need them. Most glass, paper, plastic, and metal is recyclable. When people recycle these things, it helps the environment. It saves space in landfills. (Paper takes up more space in landfills than any other thing!) And instead of wasting these materials, they get used again.

Some people have recycle bins. They put their paper, metal, glass, and plastic into the bin. A special truck takes these things to a processing center. Other people must drive to a recycling center and drop off their things.

What happens at the recycling center? Paper is shredded and then mixed with water and wood pulp to make new paper. Glass, metal, and plastics are melted down. Then they are poured into molds to form new things. Glass jars are melted down and become new glass jars. Recycling lets things be used over and over.

STORY QUESTIONS

1. Which of the following cannot be recycled?
a. dirty paper
b. dirty banana
c. plastic bag
d. soda can

2. What happens to glass jars that you throw out instead of recycle?
a. People dig through the trash, find them, and send them to a recycling center.
b. They get reused as food containers.
c. They take up space in a landfill.
d. They slowly rot and turn back into soil.

3. What is the most important reason to recycle paper?
a. It saves trees from being cut down.
b. It will keep us from running out of paper.
c. It keeps the cost of paper low.
d. A lot of people are doing it.

4. Which of the following is **true**?
a. Some people have to drive their things to a recycling center.
b. We have a lot of space available for landfills.
c. Glass takes up more space in landfills than any other thing.
d. Anything is recyclable.

DAILY Name _____ Date _____
Warm-Up 2

CITIZEN TEST

Naturalized citizens are not born in the United States or its territories. They become citizens by fulfilling certain requirements. A requirement is something needed. What are some requirements to become a naturalized citizen?

One must be at least 18 years old. One must have good moral character. If one is moral, one is good. One does not commit crimes or hurt others. One must have lived in the United States for at least five years. One must pass two tests. One test is an English test. The other is a civics test. The civics test is on American history and government.

Not all people have to meet these requirements. Sometimes there are exceptions. Children can be naturalized. They do not have to be 18 years old. They can be naturalized if their parents apply for them. Sometimes older people do not have to learn English. Exceptions are made case by case.

Which president is called "the father of our country"? How many senators are in Congress? What is the capital of your state? Where is the White House located? What do the stars on our flag mean? These five questions are from a list of 96 questions. The list is for the civics test. People can use the list to study for the test. The test they take will not have all 96 questions. The test will only have some of the 96 questions.

What are the answers to the sample questions? The first answer is George Washington. He is the "father of our country." The second answer is 100. We have 50 states. We have two senators from each state. This means we have 100 senators. There are 50 answers to the third question! Each state has a different capital. The answer to the fourth question is Washington, D.C. Our White House is located there. The last question is about our flag. There are 50 stars on the flag. Each star stands for a state. How did you do on the questions? Did you know about our government?

STORY QUESTIONS

1. This story is mainly about . . .
   a. who is a citizen.
   b. the United States.
   c. requirements for some citizens.
   d. what to study for tests.

2. How many questions are on the study list for the civics test?
   a. 18
   b. 50
   c. 100
   d. 96

3. What question would most likely be on a civics test?
   a. Who elects the president of the United States?
   b. What ocean is the biggest ocean?
   c. Do you know who invented the first car?
   d. How old are you?

4. How can a child become a naturalized citizen?
   a. Children cannot become naturalized citizens.
   b. The child learns to speak English.
   c. The child is born in the United States or its territories.
   d. The child's parents apply for the child to become a citizen.

WHAT IS A BLOG?

A blog is a page on the Internet. The term "blog" used to refer to a web log. People used web logs to list links to various websites. They shared them with others. In other words, they kept logs of places they visited on the Internet. These web logs would have links on them. The term "link" is short for "hyperlink." It's a way to connect one webpage to another. When you click on a link, a new page will open.

Over time, people began to use blogs to write personal comments and reflections. Blogs became a form of online journaling. Blogs provide a place for readers to write what they think. Ideally, others will read the blog and comment with their reactions to what they have read. This will result in an ongoing conversation. Many teachers now use blogs with their students. Some blogs just have news and information. These blogs do not usually lend themselves to comments.

People also use blogs to list, or "log," other blogs they like or their favorite websites. Often a blog will focus on a particular topic or issue. Blogs may contain links to other websites, pictures, lists, or videos. On the Internet, the blog displays the most recent entries first.

Blogs allow a group of people to communicate with each other on different topics. This allows people to create their own publishing space with information, links, and ideas they may want to share.

STORY QUESTIONS

1. You can find a blog . . .
   a. on television.
   b. in a newspaper.
   c. on the Internet.
   d. at the store.

2. A hyperlink is . . .
   a. something that cannot control itself.
   b. a way to connect two computers together.
   c. a way to connect one webpage to another.
   d. a new computer game.

3. Which type of blog usually gets fewer comments from readers?
   a. information blogs
   b. personal blogs
   c. blogs that ask readers questions
   d. blogs with links to favorite websites

4. Why would someone want to create a blog?
   a. to try to use the telephone less
   b. because the Internet won't work without it
   c. because the teacher said to
   d. to communicate with others online

Name _____ **Date** _____

COSMIC DNA SURPRISE

In the world around us we hear the letters DNA discussed. We hear them on TV. We hear them in the news. What do they mean? How do they work?

DNA is what we call the cells in our bodies that help us to grow. They are the cells that help us to have children that look like us. The shape of DNA looks a little like a braid.

Scientists thought DNA was only found in living things on the earth. They never thought they would find it in the universe outside the earth.

Not long ago, scientists were using a telescope. It was called the Spitzer Space Telescope. They saw a double helix shape. That is a shape that is <u>usually</u> found inside living things. They had never seen it in the sky.

They found out that this DNA shape in space is about 80 light years long. It is about 300 light years away from the black hole in the Milky Way. They think that it is moving at 620 miles every second. That is very fast!

Scientists think that the black hole is making the DNA turn very fast. The telescope showed them that there is DNA in other parts of the universe.

STORY QUESTIONS

1. Another way to describe DNA would be . . .
   a. donuts need ants.
   b. don't need air.
   c. cells that are square and long.
   d. cells that make us grow and help us have children that look like us.

2. Which word is a **synonym** for the word *usually?*
   a. never   c. mostly
   b. always   d. fast

3. This passage is mostly about . . .
   a. braiding DNA.
   b. a discovery of DNA in the universe.
   c. the shape of DNA.
   d. using DNA on the earth.

4. Which one of these is **NOT** true about DNA?
   a. It is found in humans.
   b. It helps us reproduce or make children that look like us.
   c. It is not found in humans.
   d. It has a shape like a braid.

DAILY
Warm-Up 5

Name _____   Date _____

COMMANDING OFFICER

Have you ever wondered why some people are so strong? Have you thought about how they do so much with their lives? When things are hard, they keep going.

Captain Chris Nunn is one of these people. When he was little, he was put up for adoption. A family in Texas adopted him. They taught him to work hard and never give up.

When he grew up, he wanted to be in the Army's Ranger School. This is a very challenging school. He had to do a lot of physical exercise, including hiking for long periods of time in the mountains. One day when he was in the mountains, a rattlesnake bit him. He was in a lot of pain, but he would not quit. Two days later he came limping out of the mountains. He passed the Ranger class.

Chris will tell you he always wants to do his best. He works as hard as he can. Sometimes people call him "Hurricane" because he gets angry if he thinks other people are not doing their best.

He became a commanding officer at age 29. Chris was working in Afghanistan in charge of many men and many thousands of dollars in army equipment. Captain Chris Nunn will keep doing his best. He hopes to make a difference in the world.

STORY QUESTIONS

1. What word or words best describe Chris Nunn?
   a. old and tired
   b. quitter
   c. never gives up
   d. young and mean

2. If Chris gave you advice, he would probably say . . .
   a. "It's not the end of the world."
   b. "Today is just another day."
   c. "Don't worry. Be happy!"
   d. "Never stop trying!"

3. How old was Chris when he became a commanding officer?
   a. 30
   b. 38
   c. 54
   d. 29

4. Another title for the passage could be . . .
   a. "Riding in the Rain"
   b. "Never Give Up!"
   c. "How to Heal a Snake Bite"
   d. "I Am the Captain"

TURNOFF WEEKS

For two different weeks each year, millions of TV and computer screens around the world are blank. They are off during Turnoff Week. More people participate every year since it began in 1994. Millions of people all over the world participate in Turnoff Week. The first Turnoff week of the year is in April and the second is in September.

Each year, U.S. kids spend less time in school than they do having "screen time," that is, watching TV and/or using the computer. In fact, the only thing they spend more time doing than viewing TV is sleeping! Studies show that kids who watch too much TV are more likely to have reading problems. The creators of Turnoff Week want us to reduce our screen time, giving us more time to "think, read, create, and do the things we never have time for."

Many kids are surprised at how much there is to do besides watch TV or play on the computer. They do puzzles, read books, and play games. They skate and ride bikes with friends. They play outdoors. Can you live without your favorite TV shows? Find out by joining this year's Turnoff Week.

STORY QUESTIONS

1. The word *participate* means . . .
    a. get out of.
    b. learn about.
    c. dislike.
    d. join in.

2. How many Turnoff Weeks are there every year?
    a. five
    b. three
    c. two
    d. four

3. According to the passage, American kids spend the most hours each week . . .
    a. playing on the computer.
    b. watching TV.
    c. sleeping.
    d. eating.

4. Which of the following is something that the creators of Turnoff Week would **NOT** want you to do during Turnoff Week?
    a. read a book
    b. play video games
    c. spend time with friends and family
    d. turn the lights on in the house

DAILY Warm-Up 7

Name _____ Date _____

WHAT THE PRESIDENT CAN'T DO

The president is a leader. In the United States, the president is elected. He or she is elected every four years. How is the president elected? People vote for a president every four years. The president leads the country. But there is one thing he or she can't do. What can't the president do?

The president can't make a new law. A law is a rule. The rules are to keep us safe. Some laws tell us what we can do. Other laws tell us what we can't do. We have laws about cars, seatbelts, schools, food, helmets, and more.

A law starts with an idea. The idea may be new. The idea may be to change an old law. Only people in Congress can make a new law. Congress has two parts. One part is the Senate. The other part is the House of Representatives. People in the Senate are called senators. People in the House are called representatives. Senators and Representatives are elected. People vote for them.

First, someone in Congress writes a bill. Second, Congress votes on the bill. The House votes on the bill. The Senate votes on the bill. The bill must pass the Senate and the House. If it passes, the bill is sent to the president. The president can sign the bill. If the president signs the bill, the bill becomes a law.

The president may veto the bill. If a bill is vetoed, it is not signed. It does not become law unless something happens. Congress must override the veto. To override the veto, Congress must vote again. Two-thirds of both the House and Senate must vote to pass the bill again. If two-thirds vote for the new rule, the bill becomes a law.

STORY QUESTIONS

1. What can't the president do?
   a. be a leader
   b. veto a bill
   c. make a new law
   d. get elected every four years

2. This story is mainly about . . .
   a. how a law is made.
   b. the Senate.
   c. the House of Representatives.
   d. how Congress can override a veto.

3. The Senate is part of . . .
   a. a bill.
   b. the House of Representatives.
   c. the president.
   d. Congress.

4. People do **not** elect . . .
   a. presidents.
   b. senators.
   c. bills.
   d. representatives.

DAILY Name _____ Date _____
Warm-Up 8

SAVING THE MOVIES

The first movies were made using black and white cameras. The film for the pictures were cut up and made into long strips. They were played on a movie projector in a theater. Today, people can see movies almost anywhere. They can see movies on computers. Others watch movies on iPods®. Some even watch movies on their cell phones. The world of movies is changing very fast.

Some filmmakers want to use digital photography for making movies. Digital photography is cheaper, takes fewer people and less space. It is easy to use and can be done in a small area. However, they do not turn out as clear as the original way of filming.

A man named Robert Rodriguez says that digital form is the new way to make movies. He says it is the way to keep movie theaters alive. He does not want them to become extinct.

Robert writes movies and shoots them. He directs them and puts them together. He even does the special effects. Robert does them all in digital format. He does this in his own home in Texas. He can make most movies for half of the money it would usually cost.

Rodriquez wants to make movies that can only be seen in theaters. His idea is to make movies, for less money, only to be shown in theaters. He feels this will help preserve the original way to watch a movie.

STORY QUESTIONS

1. What makes Robert unusual?
   a. He is trying to save the movie theaters.
   b. He is making movies.
   c. He only wants to make movies that can be shown on television.
   d. He is the only filmmaker who lives in Texas.

2. Which of these is **NOT** something positive about digital movies?
   a. They need fewer people to make them.
   b. They cost less than making movies the old way.
   c. They can be made using only a small amount of space.
   d. They are not as clear as the other kind.

3. Where can't people watch movies today?
   a. on the moon   c. on an iPod®
   b. on a cell phone   d. on a television

4. To make movies digitally you would probably use a . . .
   a. typewriter.   c. magnifying glass.
   b. computer.   d. book.

DAILY Name _____ Date _____

Warm-Up 9

HOSPITAL TECHNOLOGY

Many scientists today are trying to discover new ways to help doctors, nurses, and patients in hospitals. They are trying to create new machines that help to ease the pain of patients and make doctors' and nurses' jobs easier.

One machine that is helping patients is called a video remote interpreter, or VRI. It is a machine that helps people who are deaf. This machine connects to people outside the hospital that can help the deaf person communicate with the doctors and nurses.

Another machine is being made for people with bad burns. This machine will be set up next to the hospital bed. It will be close to, but not touching, the patient. This is important, as people with burns are often in a lot of pain. It hurts them even more to have the burns touched. Usually a doctor or nurse needs to take a <u>sample</u> of the burn. They need to get a part of the skin from the burn. They do this so they can test for infection. Getting the sample is painful for the patient. This machine will be able to test a burn for infection by using the air around the burn. It will not touch the skin of the patient.

Scientists are working every day to invent new technology for hospitals. They want to help people who are sick. They want to help people stay healthy.

STORY QUESTIONS

1. VRI stands for . . .
   a. Very Runny Ink.
   b. Very Realistic Intelligence.
   c. Virtual Running Image.
   d. Video Remote Interpreter.

2. Which word could be a **synonym** for *sample*?
   a. skin   c. arm
   b. piece   d. leg

3. Why did the scientists try to make a machine that can work near the burn patient?
   a. so it can hum for the sick person
   b. so it can make a new noise
   c. so it can read the air and check for infections
   d. so it can watch the patient

4. A VRI is used for patients who are . . .
   a. blind.   c. in a lot of pain.
   b. burned.   d. deaf.

Name _____ **Date** _____

HABITAT FOR HUMANITY

In 1976, Linda and Millard Fuller started Habitat for Humanity. This program builds houses for families that need them. The money that the family is able to pay for the needed house goes back to Habitat for Humanity. That money is then used to help build more houses. A lot of the money for the houses is paid by donations. Many people also donate their time to help build the houses. This means they do not get paid. They are called <u>volunteers</u>.

Many of the volunteers are people who build houses for a living. Some have no building experience, but still want to help. The people who are going to move into one of the houses also help build it. They work side by side with the volunteers. The frame of the house has to be built. The roof has to be put on. The walls have to be painted. Everyone puts in a lot of time hammering, painting, sawing, and gluing until the job is done.

Habitat for Humanity has built more than 300,000 houses around the world. They have helped to make life better for many people, one house at time.

STORY QUESTIONS

1. The people who live in the Habitat houses . . .
   a. pay double what they would for another house.
   b. do not help build the house.
   c. must help build the house.
   d. get the house for free.

2. According to the passage, *volunteers* are people who . . .
   a. know how to build houses.
   b. don't like to paint.
   c. families that live in houses.
   d. don't get paid.

3. How many houses has Habitat for Humanity built?
   a. over 300,000
   b. 3,000
   c. more than 3,000,000
   d. 30,000

4. We can best describe Millard and Linda as . . .
   a. people who love to save their money.
   b. people who care about helping others.
   c. people who love to buy fancy things.
   d. people who live in a big house.

AYSO SOCCER

Have you ever wanted to kick a soccer ball? Have you ever wanted to play on a soccer team? AYSO soccer may be just the place for you. It is one of the largest soccer programs in the U.S.

What does AYSO mean? AYSO stands for American Youth Soccer <u>Organization</u>. It is a club that is in all 50 states. AYSO has five simple things it believes in.

The most important idea is that everyone plays. All players must play at least half of every game. This makes them feel like they are an important part of the team. They do not have to be worried about spending most of the time sitting on the sidelines.

The second belief is to have balanced teams. Teams that play each other should be made up of players that have the same amount of experience.

The third belief of AYSO is to have open registration. This means everyone is allowed to play. As long as a child is between the ages of 4–19, he or she can play.

Positive coaching is the fourth belief. Coaches in AYSO make soccer fun as well as a learning time. Children learn how to be supportive of each other and play like a team.

The last belief is that all players should be good sports. They should respect each other. Children learn that winning is not the most important thing. Being a good sport and doing your best is what playing in AYSO is all about.

STORY QUESTIONS

1. The word *organization* means the same as . . .
   a. game.
   b. soccer ball.
   c. house.
   d. group or club.

2. Who can play in AYSO?
   a. children ages one to three
   b. children ages 4–19
   c. adults ages 40–50
   d. only girls

3. The author's purpose for this passage is . . .
   a. to entertain the reader with soccer jokes.
   b. to inform the reader about the rules of the soccer player.
   c. to persuade the reader to kick a soccer ball on weekends.
   d. to inform the reader about the five beliefs of the AYSO.

4. Which statement is **NOT** true about AYSO?
   a. Coaches are positive.
   b. Teams should be balanced.
   c. Only fantastic players get to play the game.
   d. All players must play at least half of every game.

DAILY Warm-Up 12

Name _____ Date _____

OPPORTUNITIES FOR KIDS

Have you ever wanted to help other people but thought you were too young? There are many opportunities for kids to do great things. Some of them may seem small, but they make the people being helped extremely happy.

One activity you can do is to make greeting cards for people who are in a retirement home. Many of them can no longer leave their rooms. They do not have the chance to talk to many people, and often don't get much mail. You can help <u>brighten</u> their day with a cheerful card. You might even be able to arrange for a visit with them. You can read your card to them; they may even want you to make more so they can send them to friends! You could also read your favorite book to them, or play a card game. There are many activities that seniors would love to do with someone else.

Another group of people you can help is children in hospitals. If you can sew or knit, you can make a blanket for them to snuggle if they don't have toys from home. You can visit a hospital and play board games with the children there. You might want to read picture books to the younger children.

There are many things you can do to make someone's day a little brighter. You don't need money or a lot of skills. You can make a big difference in a person's life just by being willing to donate some of your time.

STORY QUESTIONS

1. Which activity is **NOT** mentioned in the passage?
   a. making cards
   b. making blankets
   c. playing board games
   d. running races

2. A word or phrase that could mean the same as *brighten* is . . .
   a. darken.
   b. make sad.
   c. make happier.
   d. make sick.

3. The main idea of this passage is . . .
   a. the American Red cross wants you to help.
   b. no matter how much you do, you will never make a difference.
   c. kids are too young to help others.
   d. kids can help many different people.

4. Which of these could be another way kids could help out in the community?
   a. Pick up litter from alongside the road.
   b. Go on vacation.
   c. Do your regular chores at home.
   d. Steal candy bars at the grocery store.

DAILY
Warm-Up 13

Name _____

Date _____

KIDS' CLUBS

Clubs are great ways to meet people your age. They are also a way to enjoy many different exciting activities.

Girls Scouts of America is a program for girls. They can be 5–17 years in age. Girls meet every week of the school year. They learn to help out in the community. They learn to work as a team. They build life skills. They make friends. They build strong values and find out what makes them special.

Boy Scouts is for boys. Boy Scouts teach character. They teach the boys to be responsible citizens. They learn survival skills. Also, boys learn to build strong bodies. Boy Scouts are from 5–17 years old.

Awana Club is a club for both boys and girls. It is like Boys Scouts and Girl Scouts. Boys and girls from 3–17 may go to Awana. It meets every week of the school year. They learn to be responsible citizens. They do community service. They learn to build strong morals. They learn to develop character. There are contests and games each year.

Girls Scouts, Boy Scouts, and Awana Club are just three of the many types of clubs available to you. Join one today!

STORY QUESTIONS

1. What are all three clubs interested in building?
   a. strong buildings
   b. strong bodies
   c. strong values
   d. strong clubs

2. A **synonym** for the word *join* could be . . .
   a. quit.
   b. make.
   c. enter.
   d. draw.

3. The author's purpose for this passage is to . . .
   a. entertain the reader with funny, new information.
   b. inform the reader about clubs that he or she might be interested in joining.
   c. persuade the reader to attend Boy Scouts.
   d. none of the above.

4. Boy and Girl Scouts have kids from the ages of . . .
   a. 0–9.
   b. 5–17.
   c. 6–19.
   d. 5–30.

DAILY Warm-Up 14

Name _____ Date _____

JURY DUTY

Twelve people sit in a box. The box is in a courtroom. The box is a jury box. The twelve people make up a jury. Each person is a juror. Mothers and fathers may be jurors. Teachers may be jurors. Doctors may be jurors. All kinds of people can be jurors.

If a person is accused of doing something wrong, he or she has the right to a trial. If you are accused of something, you are blamed. You are charged. Sometimes a trial is needed to see if the charges are correct. One side tries to prove that the charges are correct. The other side tries to prove that the charges are not correct. Each side has lawyers. Lawyers are people who know all about laws.

A trial takes place in court. Sometimes, a judge decides if the charges are correct. Other times, the lawyers ask the judge for a trial by jury. Everyone has the right to a trial by jury if they ask. In a trial by jury, the jury decides if the charges are correct.

Letters are sent to all kinds of people. The people do many different jobs. Some people are rich. Some people are poor. All the people are U.S. citizens. All the people are at least 18 years old. The letters tell the people to come to court for jury duty. In court, lawyers talk to all the people. The jury is chosen.

The jury sits together. They sit in a jury box. They listen to all the lawyers. The judge listens, too. The judge makes sure that court rules are obeyed and that the trial is fair. After the trial, the jury goes away to talk together. No one else is there. The jury decides if the charges are correct. Sometimes it takes only 30 minutes to decide. Sometimes it takes days or even weeks!

STORY QUESTIONS

1. This story is mainly about . . .
   a. what a jury does and who makes it up.
   b. what happens when someone is charged.
   c. what lawyers do in court.
   d. what judges do when there is not a jury.

2. Who could **not** be on a jury?
   a. someone who is poor
   b. someone who is twelve years old
   c. someone who is a U.S. citizen
   d. someone who is a rich

3. What happens first?
   a. A jury is chosen.
   b. A person is charged.
   c. Letters are sent out.
   d. Lawyers ask for a trial by jury.

4. If someone is accused, they . . .
   a. sent a letter.
   b. are blamed.
   c. are chosen to be a juror.
   d. decide if the charges are correct.

FICTION

Contemporary Realistic Fiction

Mystery/Suspense/Adventure

Historical Fiction

Fantasy

Fairy Tales/Folklore

MARSHA

Marsha lived with her stepmother Minty and her father Moppy in a large mansion. Her father had his own business and was often traveling across the country. Marsha was left home with her stepmother and her two stepbrothers, Muddy and Mushy.

Every morning the boys would yell at her and put dirty socks under her bed. They would leave cookie crumbs on the floor of her bedroom. They would use their muddy shoes to track dirt all over the floors in the hallway. Their rooms would look like pigpens, and they would force Marsha to clean them before she went to school.

One day while her father was away, she and her friend Maria had a wonderful idea. They put on rubber gloves, went to the woods, and <u>gathered</u> poison ivy plants. They smeared the leaves all over the sheets of Muddy and Mushy's beds.

That evening, the boys were up to their usual mean tricks. Marsha just smiled and said, "Thanks guys, but now it's my turn."

The very next morning, the boys woke up feeling very itchy. Their mother suggested they stay home from school. They did not want to miss the baseball game, though, so they grabbed their backpacks and ran out the door.

As the day went on, they got more and more itchy. They were sent to the nurse. Muddy and Mushy had poison ivy all over their arms, legs, and bodies. The nurse sent them home for two weeks.

Marsha and Maria got them good, so they never bother Marsha again. (Well, not as much anyway!)

STORY QUESTIONS

1. Why was Marsha often left with her stepbrothers and stepmother?
   a. Her dad was on vacation in Hawaii.
   c. Her father liked to eat out.
   b. Her father was away on business.
   d. She liked being left home with them.

2. A **synonym** for *gathered* would be . . .
   a. collected.
   c. met.
   b. let loose.
   d. mixed together.

3. Why did Marsha use rubber gloves?
   a. They were good for her skin.
   b. So she and Maria wouldn't get poison ivy.
   c. They helped her with her homework.
   d. She didn't want to touch her stepbrothers.

4. This fairy tale is most like . . .
   a. "Cinderella."
   c. "Sleeping Beauty."
   b. "Three Billy Goats Gruff."
   d. "Jack and the Beanstalk."

Name _____   Date _____

THREE LITTLE ANTS

One day, three little ants—Frank, Albert, and Tommy—set out to seek their fortune. They waved goodbye to their mother and set off down the road with suitcases under their arms.

Frank, the oldest, found a nice place on a hillside to build his home. He built his out of pieces of straw he found lying on the ground. His house went up quickly, in just one day. Frank settled in and was happy.

Albert was the second oldest. He wanted to make a house that was a little <u>sturdier</u> than his brother's house. He gathered sticks, tied them all together with strong ropes, and cut windows and doors. He also made an oven out of mud, rocks, and dirt. It took him about three days to build his house, and he was happy.

The youngest brother was Tommy. Tommy was very wise and careful. He collected strong pieces of wood, cut each one carefully, and fitted the pieces together perfectly. He bought tiles for the roof and poured a cement floor. His house was the talk of the neighborhood, and he finished in two months.

One morning, Billy, the anteater, was walking around the neighborhood. He noticed the three new houses. Billy smelled ants, so he stopped to see if he could get a few to snack on. Frank's house was easy to push over; it was made of straw. Unfortunately for Billy, Frank ran out the back door to Albert's. Albert's house was a little tougher to knock over, but Billy succeeded. Albert and Frank escaped again, and Billy got sticks in his nose. Finally, he came to the last house. He sucked as hard as he could, but the three ants would not come out the front door. Instead, he got a nose full of hot sauce!

That Tommy! Billy's nose was burning. He ran away and never bothered the brothers again.

STORY QUESTIONS

1. Which words describe Tommy?
  a. mean, ugly, patient
  b. quick, hasty, lucky
  c. reckless, careless, sloppy
  d. careful, patient, smart

2. How were Albert and Frank unlike Tommy?
  a. They were both careless and lazy. Tommy was hardworking.
  b. They were both hardworking. Tommy was lazy.
  c. They were both sleepy. Tommy was wide awake.
  d. They were both interested in fireplaces. Tommy was interested in drawing.

3. In the passage, *sturdier* means . . .
  a. dirtier.   b. stronger.   c. weaker.   d. cleaner

4. This fairy tale is most like . . .
  a. "Cinderella."
  b. "Snow White and the Seven Dwarfs."
  c. "The Three Little Pigs."
  d. "Jack and the Beanstalk."

DAILY
Warm-Up 3

Name _____ Date _____

JESSIE AND THE CORNSTALK

Early one rainy morning in Iowa, Jessica's mother sent her to town with the last five dollars of cash in the house. She told her daughter to get a loaf of bread and a half-gallon of milk.

Jessica put on her blue rain jacket and blue boots. She was walking along dreaming, when she ran into Jake from school.

"What do you have in your hand, Jessie?"

"It's five dollars to buy some bread and milk."

He offered to sell Jessica some magic corn plants to make the family rich. She gave him the five dollars and went home with the plants.

When she came home, her mother was furious and sent Jessica to bed with no supper. She hurled the "magic plants" out into the cornfield and went to bed.

In the middle of the night, Jessica awoke to hear a loud banging on her window. It was a huge branch. She opened her window, grabbed her cell phone, and started climbing the stalk.

When she reached the top, she found a large castle, a friendly maid, and a sleeping giant. She noticed a suitcase full of money was lying next to the bed.

Jess grabbed the money and ran out the castle door. She called her dad on the cell phone and told him to get the ax. As she climbed down the cornstalk, her father chopped it away. When she reached the bottom, she gave him the suitcase. Their family bought their farm, and they were never hungry again.

STORY QUESTIONS

1. Which color might be Jessica's favorite?
    a. blue   c. brown
    b. orange   d. red

2. The word *hurled* in this story means . . .
    a. tossed gently.   c. threw.
    b. picked up.   d. touched.

3. What modern technology does Jessica use to reach her father?
    a. a computer   c. an iPod® nano
    b. a cell phone   d. a walkie-talkie

4. This fairy tale is most like . . .
    a. "Sleeping Beauty."   c. "The Little Red Hen."
    b. "Jack and the Beanstalk."   d. "Three Billy Goats Gruff."

Name _____ Date _____

LITTLE BROWN HUMMINGBIRD

On a farm in Kansas lived a little brown hummingbird, a blue jay, a robin, and a mean crow. The little brown hummingbird did all the work on the farm. She took care of the animals, made the meals, and took the grain to the market.

The blue jay spent each day in the kitchen, eating everything the little brown hummingbird made. Blue jay would follow her and gobble up the goodies when they came out of the oven.

The robin sat on the porch each day. He told the hummingbird that she was not fast enough with her work. He also loved to steal her fresh pies off the windowsill. He would eat them while she did the morning egg gathering.

The crow was always hanging out in the yard. He constantly pecked at the animals' food. He also loved to get the animals mad at each other. The hummingbird had to stop the fights and remind the crow to <u>mind his own business</u>.

One day, it was the hummingbird's birthday. She was tired of doing all the work and wanted to celebrate. She asked the blue jay to help, but he was too hungry. She asked the robin to help, but he was in a bad mood. She asked the crow to help, but he had to <u>bother</u> the chickens. So she made a birthday cake by herself. But, this time, when it came out of the oven, she sat down and ate the whole thing all by herself. She didn't share one crumb. Her friends were angry. They yelled at her, but she enjoyed every bite of her fresh chocolate cake.

From that day on, the other birds always helped with the chores.

STORY QUESTIONS

1. What does the phrase "mind his own business" mean?
   a. think about everything he was eating
   b. act in a play
   c. think about himself
   d. stay out of other people's way

2. A **synonym** for *bother* could be . . .
   a. disturb.   c. bake.
   b. share.   d. scream.

3. Which words best describe the hummingbird?
   a. mean and nasty
   b. hardworking and patient with others
   c. impatient and rude
   d. lazy and cruel

4. This fairy tale is most like . . .
   a. "Puss in Boots."   c. "The Little Red Hen."
   b. "The Ugly Duckling."   d. "The Little Pear Girl."

DAILY
Warm-Up 5

Name _____   Date _____

THREE SISTER SHEEP

In the mountains lived three sheep sisters. Their names were Joleen, Julia, and Jenna. Joleen was the oldest, Julia was second, and Jenna was the youngest sister. Each morning they went across the bridge to eat the delicious green grass on the other side of the mountain.

A mean wolf named John was in charge of the bridge. Each day he charged the sisters 25 cents to cross the bridge.

John was getting very rich from collecting money from the three sheep sisters. But he was also a wolf, and wolves love to eat sheep. One day he decided he wanted to eat the sisters.

Joleen returned first, walking slowly and happily. John tried to catch her and take her home for dinner. But Joleen suggested he wait for Julia because Julia would have a much sweeter taste. John let her go.

When Julia came across the bridge, John stopped her and suggested she join him for dinner. She, too, escaped, calling back, "Ask Jenna to dinner. She will be the tastiest of all of us!"

So John sat down to wait for Jenna. Soon she came across the bridge. John called out to her, "Jenna, have dinner with me."

Jenna knew what the wolf was trying to do. She pretended to go with him. But then, in a surprise move, Jenna kicked him over the edge of the bridge. He fell into the freezing water below. Because of that, he caught a terrible cold and had to stay in bed for weeks. After that, he never invited the sisters to dinner again.

STORY QUESTIONS

1. The wolf was getting rich by . . .
   a. collecting money from the sheep.
   b. selling the sheep.
   c. selling tickets for a boat ride down the river.
   d. giving 25 cents to the sheep each day.

2. Which sheep is the oldest?
   a. Julia
   b. John
   c. Joleen
   d. Jenna

3. How did Joleen keep from getting eaten by the wolf?
   a. She told him Jenna was the best sheep to eat.
   b. She told him Julia had a sweeter taste.
   c. She told him that she was too old and tough to eat.
   d. She told him she had to go home first before dinner.

4. The fairy tale this is most like is . . .
   a. "The Three Little Pigs."
   b. "The Three Billy Goats Gruff."
   c. "Sleeping Beauty."
   d. "Jack and the Beanstalk."

DAILY
Warm-Up 6

Name _____   Date _____

PENNY LOAFER AND THE THREE MONKEYS

One morning Mother, Father, and Baby Monkey woke up to see the sun shining brightly through the kitchen window. They decided it was a fabulous day for a picnic. They packed their lunch and headed out to the jungle.

Meanwhile, on the edge of the jungle, Penny Loafer was walking, too. She was singing happily as she walked along. Suddenly, she noticed a strange little hut. It had a coconut-shelled roof and jungle vines around all the windows. It was simply adorable.

She went to the door and knocked, but no one answered. Her parents had told her never to go into someone's house without asking first. But she was very curious. She opened the door and walked in.

Penny noticed three bowls of oatmeal in the kitchen. She tasted the big bowl, but there wasn't enough brown sugar in it. She tasted the medium-sized bowl. This had too much sugar. She tasted the small bowl and found it had just the right amount of brown sugar. So she ate it all up.

By now Penny was exhausted from her long walk and unusual adventure. She went to find a bed in which to lie down for a nap. The first bed she came to was <u>gigantic</u>. It felt too hard on her back. She found a medium-sized bed, but it was too soft and puffy. Then she found a small bed that was just right. She pulled the covers up and fell into a deep sleep.

Suddenly, she was awakened by the laughter of three monkeys. They were standing over her with their big eyes wide in amazement. Penny Loafer <u>screamed</u>, ran out of the cottage and all the way home. After that, she never again went into people's homes without permission.

STORY QUESTIONS

1. An **antonym** for the word *screamed* could be . . .
   a. yelled.
   c. shrieked.
   b. bellowed.
   d. whispered.

2. A **synonym** for *gigantic* could be . . .
   a. huge.
   c. small.
   b. tiny.
   d. perfect.

3. Why didn't Penny Loafer eat the father monkey's big bowl of oatmeal?
   a. It had too much sugar.
   c. She did eat it, and it was just right.
   b. It had too little sugar.
   d. She wasn't hungry.

4. This fairy tale is most like . . .
   a. "Paul Bunyan."
   c. "Goldilocks and the Three Bears."
   b. "Little Red Riding Hood."
   d. "The Three Little Pigs."

DAILY
Warll-Up 7

Name _____ Date _____

PETER AND PATTY

Peter and Patty lived with their mother and father in a small cottage at the edge of the big forest. One tragic day, their mother died.

Not long after that, their father remarried. Peter and Patty's new stepmother did not like children. She told the father to send them to an orphanage.

Their father loved Peter and Patty very much. He did not want to take them to an orphanage. He decided to tell them they were going camping in the woods. Because they had camped many times with their mother and father, Peter and Patty did not <u>suspect</u> a thing. They packed their sleeping bags, a few changes of clothes, and some food. The stepmother sent them off with a smile.

That evening their father sat with them around the campfire and told them how special they were. He reminded them how well they knew and understood survival in the woods.

The very next morning, Peter and Patty awoke to find their father gone. He had left a note wishing them well.

Peter and Patty did not know what to do. They didn't know how to get home. They started walking, hoping to find their father. They came upon a cottage made of fresh fruit and vegetables. The sweet lady who owned the cottage adopted them, fed them well, and sent them to a good school. Patty and Peter got to have rooms of their own, and they lived happily for the rest of their lives.

STORY QUESTIONS

1. Why were the children left in the woods?
   a. Their new stepmother didn't want them.
   b. They got lost.
   c. They were camping.
   d. They were playing hide and seek.

2. Why didn't the stepmother like Peter and Patty?
   a. They were very messy.   c. They teased her.
   b. They were mean to her.   d. She didn't like children.

3. A **synonym** for the word *suspect* could be . . .
   a. tattle.   c. survive.
   b. guess.   d. confess.

4. This fairy tale is most like . . .
   a. "Hansel and Gretel."   c. "The Princess and the Pea."
   b. "Jack and the Beanstalk."   d. "The Little Red Hen."

DAILY Warm-Up 8

Name _____ Date _____

SKY BLUE

In a small kingdom far away lived a beautiful princess named Sky Blue. She lived with her father and stepmother in a castle. Sky Blue's stepmother was beautiful to look at, but evil underneath. She hated Sky Blue, because she was beautiful inside and out. Also, Sky Blue was loved by all the people in the kingdom.

Each morning the stepmother would look in her magic mirror and ask the same question, "Who is the most beautiful woman in the kingdom?" The answer was always the same— "Sky Blue."

The stepmother was furious. She paid a man to kidnap Sky Blue and take her deep into the forest and leave her there. The man drove her deep into the forest, but he didn't want to leave her alone. So he took her instead to the house of seven kind lumberjacks. The lumberjacks promised to take care of her.

All went well until the stepmother discovered Sky Blue was still alive. She disguised herself as a door-to-door saleswoman and went to the home of the lumberjacks. Sky Blue, being as kind as she was, invited the saleswoman to lunch. The stepmother put poison in Sky Blue's drink. Immediately upon sipping the drink, Sky Blue fell into a deep sleep. The lumberjacks came home to find her still asleep. They couldn't wake her. They put her body in a glass box in the forest and opened it toward the sun.

A visiting prince heard of the beautiful princess. He went to look upon her beauty that very day. He kissed her lips, and she sighed with relief. Sky Blue sat up, reached for the prince, and together they rode off into the sunset.

STORY QUESTIONS

1. What did the stepmother ask the mirror each morning?
   a. "Who is the ugliest woman in the kingdom?"
   b. "Who is the richest woman in the kingdom?"
   c. "Who is the poorest woman in the kingdom?"
   d. "Who is the most beautiful woman in the kingdom?"

2. A **synonym** for *sipping* could be . . .
   a. drinking.
   b. chewing.
   c. eating.
   d. coughing.

3. How did the prince wake Sky Blue?
   a. He shook her.
   b. He kissed her.
   c. He yelled her name in her ear.
   d. He honked a horn.

4. This fairy tale is most like . . .
   a. "The Frog Princess."
   b. "The Tortoise and the Hare."
   c. "Snow White."
   d. "The Ugly Duckling."

DAILY Name _____ Date _____
Warm-Up 9

LIZARD PRINCE

One stormy morning the princess, Henrietta, was out walking in the rain. She was wearing her favorite pale green rain jacket, green gloves, and her new green rubber boots.

As she jumped in and out of puddles, one of her new rubber boots got stuck in the mud outside the castle wall. She tugged, and tugged, but the boot just sank lower. The only thing she could do was pull her foot out and hop back to the castle wearing one boot. What a sight she was! A princess hopping on one muddy boot!

Because she was used to getting her way, she started to shriek, "My favorite boot! Who will jump into the puddle and save my favorite boot?"

An ugly lizard was sleeping nearby. He heard the cries of the princess and decided to help. He dove deep into the mud and brought up the boot. He asked the princess to kiss him and promise that she would take him with her everywhere from that moment on. However, the princess thought the lizard was the ugliest creature she had seen. She took the boot and ran away, straight for the palace.

For several days she didn't see the lizard. Then one day, he appeared, sitting on her dinner plate. She shrieked and demanded he be thrown out of the castle. Her father asked what the lizard wanted. The princess had to confess that he had saved her boot, on the condition that she would take him everywhere.

Her father told her she must honor her promise. Henrietta was so angry, she threw the lizard out the window. As he hit the ground, he became a handsome prince. He told her that the <u>wicked</u> witch had put a spell on him. She was the only one who could break the spell.

Henrietta and the prince were married, and they lived happily ever after in the castle.

STORY QUESTIONS

1. What do you think is Henrietta's favorite color?
a. blue
c. green
b. red
d. purple

2. Why was the princess wearing her rain jacket, gloves, and rubber boots?
a. The weather was rainy.
c. These were her favorite clothes.
b. It was hot outside.
d. There were piles of snow to walk through.

3. Why was Henrietta going to have to keep the lizard?
a. The lizard was her friend.
b. Her father made her honor her promise.
c. She wanted to play with him.
d. He promised to give her money.

4. A **synonym** for *wicked* could be . . .
a. cruel.
c. sweet.
b. nice.
d. kind.

Name _____ **Date** _____

THE SLOTH AND THE TIGER

The race was on. All the animals of the jungle had gathered for the final showdown. They had put aside their differences for the day and were dressed in their sportiest outfits.

Signs read, "Go Sloth! You're the Boss!"

Others said, "Tiger, Tiger, he's our man. If anyone can run fast, he sure can!"

Bang! The two runners were off.

Tiger was in the lead from the very beginning, with his long strides and fast legs. Until he reached the edge of the jungle, he put on a good show for the crowd. But as soon as he stepped into the forest, he looked back and grinned. "Silly sloth, who does he think he is, trying to beat such a fast animal as me?" With that, Tiger pulled out the lawn chair he had hidden behind a tree and fell fast asleep. Sloth kept moving slowly along the path.

Several hours later, a deafening roar awoke him. The band was playing, and animals were cheering wildly. He knocked over his lawn chair and ran off in a flash. However, as he rounded the bend to the finish line, he noticed that sloth was already there. Around his neck was a shiny, gold medal. He was holding a <u>massive</u> trophy in the air.

The only thing Tiger could do was shake Sloth's hand and smile weakly.

"Congratulations, Sloth. You deserve the medal."

"Thanks," said Sloth politely. "I would sure like to take a nap in a lawn chair about now! I've had a long day!"

They both smiled.

STORY QUESTIONS

1. A **synonym** for the word *massive* could be . . .
   a. tiny.
   b. gigantic.
   c. small.
   d. little.

2. Which of the words below could be used to describe Sloth?
   a. polite
   b. mean
   c. very fast
   d. angry

3. Why did Tiger awaken from his nap?
   a. The roar of the crowd woke him up.
   b. The sound of sirens woke him up.
   c. The cry of the birds woke him up.
   d. His grandmother woke him up.

4. Which story does this remind you of?
   a. "Goldilocks and the Three Bears"
   b. "The Tortoise and the Hare"
   c. "The Little Red Hen"
   d. "How the Elephant Got Its Trunk"

Name _____ **Date** _____

GOOFY GOOSE

Gus, the goose, came into the world just as the sun peeked its head over the mountains. Mother hen noticed that one of her eggs was much larger than the rest, but that didn't bother her any. An egg was an egg, and her job was to sit on it until it hatched.

When he finally pecked his way out of the egg, Gus's mother was even more surprised. He had a long neck and a fuzzy head. His little body was round, fat, and dirty white. He didn't look anything like any of her other fuzzy, yellow chicks. But it was her job to care for her chicks, so she did.

As Gus grew, his body grew differently than his brothers' and sisters'. His neck grew so much he could barely talk to his mother unless he bent over, nearly touching the ground.

Gus talked funny, his brothers and sister thought, so they teased him. He made a honking noise rather than a chirping noise. He also walked funny, with a waddle. One day, he finally went and talked to his mother about all the jokes and mean things his brothers and sisters said.

She answered simply, "The day you were born, you were different from all of the other babies. But don't you know, Gus? You are not a chicken, but a beautiful goose!"

With that, she pointed her beak to the farm next door, and Gus noticed animals that looked just like him. A beautiful girl goose named Gerty was staring right at him.

"May I go over, Mother?" he asked.

"Certainly, and have a great time, you gorgeous goose, you!" she said as she waved.

STORY QUESTIONS

1. Why didn't the mother hen worry about the egg that was different?
  a. She was always hunting for eggs that were different.
  b. She loved bigger eggs.
  c. She liked the way it shone in the sun.
  d. Her job was to sit on an egg (any egg) until it hatched.

2. According to the passage, how was Gus different from the other chicks on the farm?
  a. He wasn't different.
  b. His eyes and nose were different.
  c. He was a boy, and the rest were girls.
  d. The way he walked and talked was different.

3. What discovery did Gus make one day?
  a. He was a goose.
  b. He was a chicken.
  c. He was too old to play in the pond.
  d. His mother was mad at him.

4. This fairy tale is most like . . .
  a. "The Three Little Pigs."
  b. "The Ugly Duckling."
  c. "The Little Red Hen."
  d. "The Frog Princess."

Name _____   **Date** _____

LITTLE BANANA GIRL

"Give me what you owe me!" demanded the king. "I want a full basket of bananas each time I pass by your house!"

"Your Majesty, the crop has not been good. I only have a small basket of bananas."

"I will be back at 5 P.M., and I want a large basket!" bellowed the king.

Ashley's father <u>sadly</u> shook his head. No matter what he did there would never be enough bananas by 5 P.M.

Ashley, being the smart child she was, offered a solution. She suggested that her father hide her in the bottom of the basket, and then cover her with bananas. This would save the family from the anger of the king. She told her father that she would keep in touch with the family as best she could. Her father finally gave in. He placed her in the basket, and covered her with bananas.

At exactly 5 P.M., the king returned. He was pleased to find a basket full of bananas. As he drove off, the father looked on sadly. But he smiled to think of the surprise that would be waiting for the king when he went to use the bananas in the basket.

The servants quickly discovered the basket trick. They hid the girl in the maid's room. Ashley did well in the castle. All of the servants adored her, as did the king's son, Prince Patrick.

The king was informed, one sad day, of the trick Ashley's family had played on him. He was so angry that he sent her to kill a dragon in another land. He figured she would never return. But Ashley accomplished the chore. She returned with the dragon's head. The king told her that whatever she wished would be hers.

She asked for a basket of bananas. However, the prince made the servants place him in the bottom of the basket. He was secretly in love with Ashley. When the trick was discovered, the king had to allow his son to marry Ashley. They lived happily ever after with bananas each week, from their own trees on the palace grounds.

STORY QUESTIONS

1. What was Ashley's solution to her father's problem?
 a. She told her father to hide from the king.
 b. She hid in the basket so it would look like there were a lot of bananas in it.
 c. She and her father hid under the basket of bananas.
 d. She told the king that they had already given him a basket of bananas.

2. Ashley could be described as . . .
 a. ugly and mean.
 c. smart and determined.
 b. selfish and cruel.
 d. jealous and thin.

3. An **antonym** for the word *sadly* could be . . .
 a. miserably.
 c. gloomily.
 b. unhappily.
 d. joyfully.

4. Why did the prince hide in the basket that the king gave to Ashley?
 a. He wanted to run away from his father.
 b. He was secretly in love with Ashley.
 c. He wanted it to look like there were a lot of bananas in the basket.
 d. He wanted to see where Ashley lived.

DAILY Warm-Up 13

Name _____ Date _____

WHY ANTS BITE LEGS AT PICNICS

Nearly every Saturday, a family of five would spend the entire day at the park. The mother, father, two boys, and a girl loved having picnics in the park. They also enjoyed riding bikes, playing, and feeding the ducks that swam in the pond.

However, there was one problem. In the park lived <u>a colony of ants</u>. Each day they would look for food. Each of them did his or her own job. Everything was fine, until the family started coming to the park.

While their parents and sister were getting the picnic basket unloaded, Jeremy and James would look for anthills. Once they found them, they would put in small sticks of dynamite. They would light the fuse, and then BOOM! The two boys loved to see the ants scatter and run for their lives. They rolled on the ground as the adult ants were thrown high into the air, and the babies were tossed another way. They were terrible and mean.

One day, as the ants watched the boys sit down on a blanket for lunch, they made a plan. They called other ants for miles around. They all hid under the blanket on which the family was sitting.

Suddenly, screams could be heard all across the park. The ants were attacking James and Jeremy. Ants of all shapes and sizes swarmed on Jeremy's and James's legs as they sat on the blanket. The ants bit hard. The boys yelled and slapped, but the ants continued to march and bite. Finally, when the boys' legs were puffy and <u>swollen</u>, the queen ant led the ants back to her hill. <u>Mission accomplished</u>. From this day forward, the boys never bothered them again . . . or they got bites as souvenirs.

So if an ant ever bites you, you have Jeremy and James to thank!

STORY QUESTIONS

1. "A colony of ants" is another way of saying . . .
   a. a boatload of ants.
   b. a wagonload of ants.
   c. a basketful of ants.
   d. a group of ants.

2. Jeremy and James could be described as . . .
   a. kind and thoughtful.
   b. gentlemen.
   c. troublemakers.
   d. angels.

3. "Mission accomplished" means . . .
   a. the space mission was underway.
   b. the task was completed.
   c. the astronauts have landed.
   d. get ready for the mission to Mars.

4. A **synonym** of *swollen* could be . . .
   a. shrunk.
   b. bitten.
   c. red.
   d. enlarged.

DAILY
Warm-Up 14

Name _____ Date _____

BEETLE BOY AND THE TALKING COCONUT

Beetle Boy was known all over the jungle as a prankster. He was always playing tricks on the other animals, even if it hurt their feelings. He didn't care. He was having too much fun to stop.

One day, while he was playing in a coconut tree, he noticed Pinky the parrot flying overhead. Beetle Boy dived inside the nearest coconut and began one of his tricks.

"Hey, dumb bird. Why are your wings so funny? Why are you flying so slowly?"

Pinky looked around, but all he could see were coconuts. One coconut kept calling to him and making rude remarks.

He went up to the tree and picked it up. "I will take you to see the king of the jungle. Let's see if you talk to him this way. He will be pleased to have a coconut that can talk."

When the king of the jungle, George the Great, saw the coconut and heard the story, he didn't believe it could talk. He whispered to the coconut, and then shouted at it, but it would not answer. George the Great was becoming angry. He lifted the coconut and threw it with all his might. It cracked, and out ran Beetle Boy.

Pinky and the king smiled. So, Beetle Boy was behind all this noise!

"Beetle Boy," said George the Great. "I declare that you will work for me in the coconut trees for the rest of your life. Without pay."

From that day on, the joke was on Beetle Boy. He worked in the coconut trees with no pay and was only given bread and water. He was never allowed to play tricks again.

STORY QUESTIONS

1. Who was George the Great?
   a. the queen of the castle
   b. the king of the jungle
   c. the jester of the palace
   d. the king of the banana trees

2. Beetle Boy is . . .
   a. mean and full of mischief.
   b. generous and giving.
   c. kind and thoughtful.
   d. helpful.

3. What was Beetle Boy's punishment?
   a. He had to work in the banana trees and eat coconuts for all meals.
   b. He had to work in the coconut trees for free and eat bread and water.
   c. He had to work hard in the castle.
   d. He had to eat coconuts for the rest of his life.

4. Which of the following is **NOT** true of Beetle Boy?
   a. He liked to play tricks on others.
   b. He made fun of other animals.
   c. He was a good friend to everyone.
   d. He pretended to be a talking coconut.

SPEEDING SPIDER

As the sun was setting low in the sky, Camel was munching on some grass when he noticed Spider running past. "Something must be wrong," he thought. "If Spider is running, I should be running, too." So he started to run after Spider.

Fox was sitting and watching the sunset. He saw Spider and Camel race by. He thought something must be wrong. He decided to run after Spider and Camel.

Rabbit was in his kitchen cutting fresh vegetables. He noticed Camel out the window. He called Snake on his cell phone. Snake called Roadrunner and Quail on walkie-talkies. Quail called Hedgehog on the house phone.

Before long, Rabbit, Snake, Roadrunner, Quail, and Hedgehog were running madly after Fox, Camel, and Spider.

Hedgehog started to get tired of all the running. He was having trouble breathing and keeping up with the rest of the animals. He called out to Fox. "Fox, why are we running?" Fox asked Snake, and Snake asked Roadrunner. None of the animals knew the answer to the question. Finally, Camel asked Spider.

"Spider, why are we running?"

Spider looked back and smiled. "I don't know why you are running, but I am late for dinner!"

STORY QUESTIONS

1. Why was Fox running?
   a. He saw his friends were running.
   b. He was late for a football game.
   c. He needed exercise.
   d. He wanted to get to school on time.

2. What technology did the animals use to communicate with each other?
   a. computers and cell phones
   b. a BlackBerry® and e-mail
   c. cell phones and walkie-talkies
   d. TVs and cell phones

3. Why was Hedgehog tired of running?
   a. He would rather be swimming.
   b. He was having trouble breathing and couldn't keep up with the rest of the animals.
   c. He wanted to do a relay race instead.
   d. His legs were shorter than the rest of the animals' legs.

4. What lesson can we learn from these animals?
   a. Don't just follow the crowd, understand why you are doing something.
   b. Always get your parents' permission before you go to a friend's house.
   c. Always call your parents if your plans change.
   d. Never talk to strangers.

DAILY Warm-Up 16

Name _____ Date _____

PRINCE AND THE PEBBLE

Once upon a time there was a princess who wanted to marry a prince. She only wanted to marry a real prince. She traveled all over the world to find one. But it was always too difficult to tell which ones were really real.

Finally, she returned home exhausted. The weather was stormy, and she was worn out from all the traveling. She sat down in front of the warm fire. Next to her were her mother, the queen, and her father, the king. They talked with sadness about the difficulty in finding a real prince.

Suddenly, the doorbell on the castle startled them. "Who could be out on such a terrible night?" thought the princess.

The princess rushed to the door. Without thinking, she threw open the door and discovered a soggy, wet traveler.

He asked if she might be the princess who was searching for a prince. She admitted she was.

"Your prince has arrived," he said simply. He brought a box of chocolates from underneath his soggy cloak.

The king, queen, and princess were not convinced, although the stranger was definitely charming. They decided to give him a test to see if what he said were true.

The queen went to the guestroom and put a small pebble underneath twenty mattresses and forty quilts. She showed the prince to the room and told him he could spend the night there.

In the morning, they asked how he slept.

"Horribly," he said. "There was something under my mattresses. I feel as if I have bumps and bruises all over."

"Congratulations. You are truly a prince," said the queen. "Now, where are those chocolates?"

STORY QUESTIONS

1. Why was the princess so sad?
   a. She had just finished a long race around the world.
   b. She couldn't find a real prince to marry.
   c. She had been out in the rain for hours.
   d. She was tired of hearing ringing doorbells.

2. Whose idea was it to put the pebble under the mattresses?
   a. the maid   c. the king
   b. the princess   d. the queen

3. In what order are we introduced to the characters?
   a. princess, queen, king, prince   c. queen, king, prince, princess
   b. prince, queen, princess, king   d. prince, king, queen, princess

4. This fairy tale is most like . . .
   a. "Little Red Riding Hood."   c. "The Princess and the Pea."
   b. "The Frog Princess."   d. "Humpty Dumpty."

Fiction: Historical Fiction

Name __Peyton__   Date __4/18__

THE TIME MACHINE

"Wow! Would you take a look at this?" Pedro climbed out the metal door of the time machine. Juan, his best friend, was close behind him. Just this morning, he had started the shiny, silver machine for the first time. Neither boy had believed it would actually work.

"Check it out! There are men in small sleds everywhere!" yelled Juan. Both boys looked around. Husky dogs and homemade sleds were everywhere, as far as the eye could see. The sleds were made of rough, brown wood and deer antlers. Eight large, sleek dogs were pulling each sled. Glancing around, the boys noticed the land was covered with brilliant, white snow.

"Where are we?" asked Pedro. "It looks like we might be in Alaska. Could we have landed in the middle of an Inuit dogsled race?"

Without warning, a sled shot past them, swaying dangerously. "Move! Outta my way!" they thought they heard the driver shout as the dogsled passed in front of them. Pedro and Juan bolted for the time machine. As they closed the door, they peered through the window watching the racers glide across thick ice. Pedro glanced at the information panel: Inuits. Alaska. 1,000 B.C. Glancing at his watch, he realized it was nearly 5:00 P.M. He flipped a switch. The time machine began whirring. Away from the Inuit dogsled race they spun, arriving home just in time for dinner!

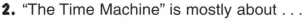

STORY QUESTIONS

1. In what did the boys travel?
   a. a time machine   c. a car
   b. a dogsled   d. a kayak

2. "The Time Machine" is mostly about . . .
   a. watching a dolphin race in Florida.
   b. making sure to be home in time for dinner.
   c. feeling the cold air in Alaska.
   d. watching a dogsled race in Alaska.

3. The purpose of this passage is . . .
   a. to entertain the reader with silly stories of sled racing.
   b. to inform the reader about Inuit dogsledding.
   c. to persuade the reader to experience time travel.
   d. to insist that the reader enter a sled race.

4. What is another word that could be used for *glanced?*
   a. looked   c. marched
   b. played   d. paraded

KWAKIUTL

"Hey Juan, I was just reading about the Kwakiutl Indians. Do you want to <u>grab another ride</u> in the time machine? Since it's Saturday, we can pack a lunch and stay all day."

Lights flashed on the time machine as Pedro and Juan strapped in. "Tell me about the Kwakiutl. What will we see?" questioned Juan.

"They lived in Canada around 1890. Salmon was their food of choice. They had canoes made of wood, and they even carved totem poles. I can't wait to find out if all this information is true!"

Beep. Beep. Whir. The time machine came to a soft landing. Pedro, an amazing pilot, had landed them right in the middle of a thick forest. They were right next to a large totem pole. As the door opened, they heard music and laughter. Ducking behind the colored totem pole, they watched the villagers dance around the fire.

Directly in front of them was a long house made of split logs. Some of the boards appeared to be missing on the roof, and smoke was billowing out of the hole in the roof.

"The women must be smoking salmon for a feast," whispered Pedro. "I want a taste of that!" Pedro, in a trance, began to walk toward the lodge.

The dancers stopped and watched in amazement as a strange boy walked up the path leading to the lodge. Juan grabbed Pedro and shoved him roughly into the time machine. Fortunately, he'd seen Pedro fly it and remembered the correct buttons to press. Whir. Beep. Buzz.

As Pedro stared out the window he sighed, "So close, and yet so far. I just wanted to taste one bite of freshly-smoked salmon!"

Juan reached in his pocket and grinned, "You can dream about salmon all night long, but I'm sure none of the dancers knew what to make of our time machine. However, I did use my knife to cut off a piece from the totem pole, and I am taking it home as a souvenir!"

STORY QUESTIONS

1. What Indian group did the boys visit?
  a. Inuit
  b. Kwakiutl
  c. Navajo
  d. Cheyenne

2. In the passage, what does the phrase "grab another ride" mean?
  a. go on another adventure
  b. get tickets for rides at the fair
  c. hold on tight
  d. get on a horse

3. Juan probably pulled Pedro back into the time machine because . . .
  a. he was afraid of what might happen if they stayed any longer.
  b. he was in a hurry to go to another place.
  c. he was hungry for lunch and wanted to fly to a restaurant.
  d. the totem pole was about to fall on the time machine.

4. Juan did not have trouble getting the time machine started because . . .
  a. he had studied time machines in school.
  b. there was a phone on the wall to call home and ask.
  c. he was sure that it would start by itself.
  d. he had paid attention when Pedro had flown it in the past.

DAILY
Warm-Up 3

Name _____ **Date** _____

CHEYENNE

"Look out!" bellowed Pedro.

A huge buffalo was right below them. Juan pulled back on the gears with all his might, but not in time to stop the time machine from hitting the back of a hairy buffalo. It was his first time driving alone, and he was feeling a bit weak in the knees.

As soon as the machine ground to a halt, Pedro and Juan scrambled to see if they had hurt the buffalo. It lay on the ground without moving.

Without warning, Pedro and Juan were surrounded by warriors. They were shouting in an unknown language. They had bows and arrows; horses were on the hill nearby. Neither boy could understand one word that was being said. They stood <u>paralyzed with fear</u>.

The warriors took the boys off to a nearby camp. They dragged the buffalo with them. When the boys saw the camp, it looked like Cheyenne camps from the books back home. As the buffalo was cut apart and the body parts were used in different ways, Juan and Pedro made signals to each other with their eyes. They continued to watch. Meat was cooked, strips were hung on a drying rack, and bones were cleaned to make sleds and needles. Fat from the animal was added to berries and nuts to make savory treats. The skin was used for clothing, tipis, and moccasins.

As evening approached, both boys continued to sit quietly, taking in all of the events of the day. The Cheyenne brought them meat, special moccasins, and a drink in a wooden cup.

"I think we are being honored as great warriors," said Pedro.

"Imagine that. I crash the machine into a buffalo, and we become warriors receiving presents! Good thing they don't know the truth about my driving skills!" admitted Juan.

Both boys nearly fell over with laughter. They settled back to enjoy the feast of the buffalo and the smiles of newfound friends.

STORY QUESTIONS

1. Based on the text, the best definition of "paralyzed with fear" would be . . .
    a. a feeling of excitement.
    c. very joyful.
    b. tremendously happy.
    d. extremely scared.

2. The Cheyenne used buffalo skins for . . .
    a. making tipis, moccasins, and clothes.
    c. making needles.
    b. cooking meat.
    d. savory treats.

3. The fat from the buffalo was useful for . . .
    a. making canoes.
    c. creating treats made with berries and nuts.
    b. taking baths in the river.
    d. shampoo.

4. Why did the Cheyenne think that Pedro and Juan were great warriors?
    a. They knew how to ride horses.
    c. They could shoot arrows very far.
    b. They had killed a buffalo.
    d. They wore the clothes of great warriors.

NAVAJO LANDING

Pedro looked at his friends, Mary and Tiffany. "Are you two ready for a sweet ride?"

"Yes," they both whispered softly.

Pedro had let both girls in on the secret of the time machine because Juan had been sick with the flu for nearly one week now. He had encouraged Pedro to take their friends and continue traveling. Tiffany had brought her video camera, and Mary was armed with a notepad, pen, and digital camera. However, they still weren't sure that the boys' stories were accurate or even true.

Whir. Blip. Beep. Lights flashed, sirens blared, and the machine sped into action. "We're moving!" gasped Mary, grasping her seatbelt until her knuckles were white.

Before they realized what was happening, they were flying into the bright sunlight. Below the machine was a red, mud-covered building.

"That's a hogan," whispered Pedro. "People lived in them for hundreds of years. They have no windows. They are cool in the summer and warm in the winter. Come on. I want to show you my favorite part of this village!"

All three kids walked to the end of the village. Pedro poked his head into a hogan and smiled. The man inside smiled back.

"He's the medicine man. He also makes sand paintings." Pedro motioned to the girls as he entered the hogan, dropping to his knees. The old man, without speaking, handed him several different bowls with brightly-colored sand in each one. Sand painting lessons had begun.

STORY QUESTIONS

1. Why does Pedro use the time machine?
   a. to see places in the past
   b. to meet his parents
   c. to get to a restaurant
   d. to run away

2. What do think will most likely happen next?
   a. The girls will learn to draw pictures with berry juice.
   b. The girls will run away.
   c. Pedro and the girls will learn tips on working with colored sand.
   d. Pedro will take a lunch break.

3. If Mary wrote an entry in her dairy, she might write . . .
   a. "Today my friends and I had an amazing adventure with the Navajo."
   b. "Today I was bored to tears."
   c. "Today it was raining cats and dogs."
   d. "Today I went to visit Juan when he was sick."

4. Why were the kids in the hogan with the medicine man?
   a. He was an enemy.
   b. He was going to teach them to sand paint.
   c. They were feeling ill.
   d. They wanted to have an adventure.

Name _____ **Date** _____

WAMPANOAG

"Fasten your seat belts!" screamed Pedro. "This is our last adventure with time travel. Dad says he is turning my machine into scrap metal, and I have to become a normal kid."

"Boo!" the other kids yelled. "Where are we headed anyway?"

"To the land of the Wampanoag."

"Who are they, and what makes them important?"

"The Wampanoag were called the 'true people of the land.' They lived in Massachusetts and Rhode Island. If they hadn't taught the Pilgrims about growing food in harsh winters, our country would not be where it is today. We owe a great deal to the Wampanoag people."

With Pedro at the wheel, the time machine landed smoothly in the middle of a cornfield. Mary climbed out and a pebble <u>grazed</u> her forehead. "Ouch, that hurt!" She looked up just in time to see two little girls giggle and run off down the path.

"Don't worry," assured Pedro. "They never meant to hurt you. The girls were most likely aiming for an old crow. Woman and girls of this culture have to throw pebbles and small sticks to keep them away from the corn. That is one of their jobs."

"What else do girls do around here?"

"Lots of chores. Picking corn, beans, and fruit are just a few of their daily chores. After that, they cut up the fruit and veggies, dry them, and make meals. Finally, they learn to weave cloth and make clothes from the skins of animals. Girls have to work all the time here."

"We've seen enough!" screeched both girls. "Take us home to our own rooms, magazines, CD players, and blue jeans!"

STORY QUESTIONS

1. What lessons did the girls learn about the Wampanoag in this story?
   a. The life of a Wampanoag girl was filled with never-ending chores.
   b. Life was easy in the Wampanoag village.
   c. Life was filled with fun and games.
   d. Winters were for planting seeds.

2. What does Pedro possess?
   a. a can of soda
   b. a watch
   c. a broad knowledge of Native American cultures
   d. a sleeping bag and pillow

3. In this story, what does the word *grazed* mean?
   a. to run a cool cloth across
   b. to chew slowly, like a cow chews his cud
   c. to hit slightly
   d. to run quickly

4. Why did the girls want to return home so quickly?
   a. They didn't want to be left behind.
   b. They were fearful the machine would break down.
   c. They missed their parents.
   d. Modern life was much more appealing.

DAILY Warm-Up 6

Name _____ Date _____

MAYFLOWER ADVENTURE

"So, Juan, where do you want to go?" Even though they had promised Pedro's dad, Juan and Pedro couldn't resist one last trip in the time machine.

"My first choice would be the *Mayflower*, either in the ocean or when they landed."

Lights flashed and the engine sputtered. Both boys looked at each other. Maybe his dad had been right; you can't have a good thing last forever.

Touchdown. Splash. Ocean water. Juan and Pedro got into the lifeboat attached to the time machine. They opened the hatch and pushed off. As the waves pounded their boat, they searched on the horizon.

Dead ahead of them was a large boat. Could it be the *Mayflower*? Juan hardly dared to hope, but Peter hoped out loud.

"It's the *Mayflower*! Wave your arms wildly! Splash loudly, maybe they will notice us!"

As it approached, they saw many sailors on the large wooden ship. One was repairing a torn sail; another was high up on the rigging, looking out to sea.

"It surely looks crowded," said Pedro. "I heard the *Mayflower* had over a hundred passengers."

"All I see are sailors," said Juan. "Most of the passengers on the *Mayflower* stayed in the ''tween decks' below. I can't imagine being in such a dark, cramped space for such a long time. They sailed for 66 days! Plus, they had no fresh food to eat, just biscuits and fish stew. Maybe oatmeal."

"Uggh," said Pedro, as the large boat pulled alongside them. "Maybe we should have listened to my dad!" Both boys shivered. They were relieved that they were about to get rescued, but were <u>horrified</u> to remember that their time machine was no longer working. How were they going to get home?

STORY QUESTIONS

1. What had the boys done without permission?
   a. gone to the beach
   b. bought sugary snacks
   c. called a friend
   d. used the time machine

2. "'Tween decks" probably means . . .
   a. teenagers on a ship.
   b. underneath the bottom of a ship.
   c. on the top deck of a ship.
   d. between decks of a ship.

3. What lesson did the boys learn?
   a. Dads might know something after all.
   b. Dads don't like to use time machines.
   c. Dads are mean on the weekends.
   d. Dads don't want you to have any fun.

4. An **antonym** for *horrified* could be . . .
   a. frightened.
   b. afraid.
   c. shocked.
   d. calm.

Name _____ Date _____

PATRICK HENRY'S INFLUENCE

"I do not know what course others may take, but as for me, give me <u>liberty</u> or give me death!"

These words kept <u>ringing</u> in my ears as I lay upon my bed. For days we had been arguing in Congress about the British, their rule, and taxes they always imposed on us. We wanted, as the thirteen Colonies, to be free to rule ourselves.

There are so many things that he said that made sense. Should we keep our opinions to ourselves for fear that we might make someone angry? Are we running out of time to wait and keep thinking things over and over? Is it not time for us to think about the struggle to be free? Is that thinking going on inside of people in all the thirteen Colonies? Don't we want to make our own laws and run our own government, the way we see best? Why should we have to pay taxes for everything from tea to paper to a country we don't even like any more?

Suddenly, I sat up. I knew what my heart was telling me. We had to go to war. Patrick Henry was right. If you believe strongly in freedom, there is only one way to get it. We must fight for liberty, or at least die trying!

As I lay back down on the pillow, a thought came to me. "Tomorrow I must tell Patrick how much I appreciate his courage to speak the words so many of us have thought, but have been too scared to speak."

STORY QUESTIONS

1. In the passage, *ringing* most likely means . . .
   a. sounding like the ringing of a bell.
   b. repeating over and over.
   c. speaking softly.
   d. shouting.

2. A **synonym** for *liberty* in the passage could be . . .
   a. slavery.
   b. taxes.
   c. freedom.
   d. death.

3. The line that made Patrick Henry the most famous was . . .
   a. "Give me no taxes or give me death!"
   b. "If we believe in freedom strongly, there is only one way to get it."
   c. "Give me liberty or give me death!"
   d. "We must go to war!"

4. The author of this passage was most likely . . .
   a. an enemy of Patrick Henry.
   b. a friend of Patrick Henry.
   c. a person living in England.
   d. a person from Patrick Henry's high school.

DAILY Warm-Up 8

Name _____ Date _____

GEORGE WASHINGTON'S LETTER

My dearest Martha,

As I am working here in Philadelphia, I am recalling several events in my life which have kept me pursuing my dreams. These, of course, are the dreams of freedom from England and the establishing of the 13 Colonies as a new nation.

As I think back to 1754, I remember it as clearly as if it had happened yesterday. This was at the beginning of one of the small fights that grew into the French and Indian War. There was fighting all around us that day, but somehow I managed to escape. I realized later that four bullets had ripped through my coat. I had to sew these up by hand. I admit I am not as skilled in sewing as you are, my dear. Also, on the very same day, two horses were shot from under me. Once again, I escaped unhurt. That day has reminded me of the importance of fighting for what I believe.

Another memory, which is vivid in my mind, is the time I spent with you on our plantation. I remember managing the lands and working alongside our workers. This memory brings me great joy. It is peaceful and reminds me of the peace we long for.

Each event, my dear, had made me what I am today. I am strong because you believe in me and in the cause. I am strong because I have survived unusual events. The fight may be long, but the victory will be sweet.

Your most humble servant,

George

STORY QUESTIONS

1. According to the passage, what brought George Washington joy?
   a. the memory of fighting in the French and Indian War
   b. the memory of working on his plantation
   c. the memory of living in Washington
   d. writing to his wife

2. This letter is written to George's . . .
   a. daughter.   c. wife.
   b. grandmother.   d. son.

3. What did George have to sew himself, even though sewing was generally done by woman?
   a. He had to sew up bullet holes in his coat.
   b. He had to sew buttons on his shirt.
   c. He had to sew an American flag.
   d. He had to sew a new hat for himself.

4. What lessons had George learned?
   a. to fight for taxes and fight for money
   b. to get what you want no matter who you hurt
   c. to look at what others have and try to get it for himself
   d. to fight for what he believed and to be thankful for what he had

DAILY Warm-Up 9

Name _____ Date _____

THOMAS JEFFERSON'S DAY OFF

"Good morning, Mr. President."

"Good Morning, Victor."

"Mr. President, today is a holiday. I was wondering if you would like anything special today?"

"Yes, Victor, as a matter of fact I would. Pancakes with maple syrup would make a good breakfast. For lunch, I'd like to have spoon bread, boiled vegetables, and ice cream. For dinner tonight, you can surprise me with something unusual."

"That will be fine, Mr. President. Are there any special activities you might like to do to relax today, before you go back to work tomorrow?"

"Certainly. I'd like to take my daughter for a ride in the carriage. I would also like to play my violin for about an hour, undisturbed, of course. I will go fishing down by the river, and then take a small walk down the avenue in front of the White House. Could you arrange that?"

"Certainly, Sir. It sounds like a relaxing day. I will make the arrangements, Sir."

"That would be <u>fabulous</u>, Victor."

"It is my job to make your life comfortable, Sir."

"Great. And Victor, one more thing."

"What is it, Mr. President?"

"Since it is a holiday, and we are <u>taking a break from the regular routine</u>, why don't you take a break and call me Thomas, instead of Mr. President or Sir."

"Yes, Sir. I mean, Thomas, Sir."

STORY QUESTIONS

1. Which is **NOT** a food the president enjoyed?
   a. pancakes
   b. vegetables
   c. microwave waffles
   d. spoon bread

2. Why does Thomas Jefferson ask to have one hour where he is not disturbed?
   a. so he can feed the ducks
   b. so he can ride in his carriage
   c. so he can play his violin
   d. so he can put his feet up in the oval office

3. "Taking a break from the regular routine" probably means . . .
   a. breaking dishes.
   b. do things in an unusual way, out of the ordinary.
   c. spending time outside.
   d. going on a vacation to a new state.

4. An **antonym** for the word *fabulous* in the passage could be . . .
   a. amazing.
   b. wonderful.
   c. awful.
   d. marvelous.

Name _____   Date _____

PAUL REVERE'S STORIES

We all loved to sit and hear the stories that my father had to tell. They were always interesting and full of adventure.

From the time he was a little boy, Papa was always looking for more to see, more to hear, and more to do than he had time to complete. His mother stayed at home with Paul and his sister, Deborah. Their father was a silversmith. When he was 15, his father died. Papa had to take over the family business. He learned to make spoons, shoe buckles, candleholders, and much more. One time he even made a collar out of silver for our neighbor's pet squirrel!

All through his life, Papa continued to experience many things. The bravest of all was the night that he rode for the freedom of our country. It was Papa's job to warn the citizens if the British were arriving by land or sea. If by sea, there would be two lanterns hanging in the top of the church tower. If they were coming by land, there would be one. That very night, there were two lanterns in the tower, so he got on his horse and rode with his coattails flying.

He rode through the villages, warning everyone about the arrival of the British. The best part, however, is that afterwards, he came home safely to us.

STORY QUESTIONS

1. Who is telling this story?
   a. a neighbor
   b. one of Paul Revere's children
   c. his wife
   d. a friend of the family

2. What is one thing that Paul Revere would **NOT** have made as a silversmith?
   a. forks, spoons, and knives
   b. window frames
   c. rings
   d. necklaces

3. How many siblings did Paul Revere have?
   a. five: Danny, Donald, Duke, Deborah, and Delia
   b. three: Deborah, Donald, and Danny
   c. one: Deborah
   d. zero

4. If the British were attacking by land, what should be hung in the church steeple?
   a. two lanterns
   b. one lantern
   c. three lanterns
   d. a map of where the British were

MARTHA WASHINGTON'S PARTY

"Abigail, would you like to sit on the right side of the table at the dinner tonight?" The head waitress, Matilda, looked at her expectantly. She was getting the table prepared for the dinner party that night at Mount Vernon.

"That would be lovely. I always enjoy sitting by Martha. She is so cheerful and kind. It seems she always turns bad events into good with laughter."

"You're right. Just this afternoon she is meeting with children who have very little in the way of material goods. They are having a picnic on the lawn."

"Yes, they are. I shall be <u>assisting</u> her with the games for that event."

"Do you think she would like me to help serve, as well?"

"I think she has it all planned out. She is a born organizer. But I am sure that she wouldn't say no to anyone who wants to lend an extra hand."

"I shall go ask her then. Will you please excuse me?"

Matilda hurried off to ask Martha's permission to help with the party for the children on the lawn.

Abigail, on the other hand, hurried back inside to create surprises of her own. Martha was always doing favors for her, making her laugh, and acting as a true friend. It was her turn to surprise Martha. She got things ready while Martha was occupied with the preparations for the party outside.

STORY QUESTIONS

1. Why did Abigail stay inside, when Matilda went outside?
  a. She did not want to help with the party.
  b. She was allergic to the flowers outside.
  c. She was planning a surprise for Martha.
  d. She was setting the table.

2. According to this passage, who was Martha Washington's good friend?
  a. Laura   c. Abigail
  b. Matilda   d. Martha

3. *Assisting* is a **synonym** for . . .
  a. caring.   c. swimming.
  b. picnicking.   d. helping.

4. How do you think Martha's friends might describe her?
  a. mean and sloppy   c. sad and lonely
  b. cheerful and organized   d. mad and impatient

DAILY Name _____ Date _____
Warm-Up 12

FLORENCE NIGHTINGALE'S VISIT

"It's the lady with the lamp," breathed the soldier as he lay on his bed in the dirty hospital in Turkey.

"I can see her," whispered the soldier next to him. "I hope she gets to us very soon. My leg hurts so badly."

"They say she was born on May 12, 1820, to British parents as they were traveling in Italy. They were very rich, you know. I think they named her after the city of Florence, because she is so beautiful. Just like that city."

"Yeah, I heard that, too. Did you know that her parents told her she couldn't be a nurse? She chose to do it anyway. She gathered up a bunch of nursing friends and came over here to Turkey to help us in the Crimean War."

"They say she is amazing. She hasn't married so far. I think she never will. The hospitals have gotten cleaner since she arrived, but the male doctors seem to be pretty upset that she is here to help."

"Well, I don't know about you, but I am glad she is here. Florence is beautiful. Look! She's headed this way."

"I'm tired, I'll just rest my eyes and wait for her to arrive. Although it is late, she'll make it to us tonight."

STORY QUESTIONS

1. Even though her family was British, why was Florence born in Italy?
   a. Her parents didn't want her to be born in Britain.
   b. Her parents were traveling in Italy.
   c. Her parents were away on business.
   d. Her parents were angry with the British government.

2. What did Florence want to do when she grew up?
   a. be a travel agent and see the world   c. be a pilot and fly planes
   b be a doctor and build hospitals   d. be a nurse and help others

3. Which is **NOT** something Florence did?
   a. She became a nurse to help soldiers fighting in Turkey.
   b. She brought a lot of her nursing friends to Turkey with her.
   c. She made hospitals cleaner and safer.
   d. She got married.

4. In the passage, Florence Nightingale is called . . .
   a. "the lady with the scissors."   c. "the lady with clean bandages."
   b. "the lady with the lamp."   d. "the lady with buried treasure."

MOTHER TERESA'S RIDE

One night I had a dream. The train I was riding in was traveling to the mountain town of Darjeeling in India. As I looked around, there were many interesting faces, young and old, on the train.

One face caught my attention. I looked again. The woman's face was old and weather-beaten. She was wearing a plain white sari with blue trim. A small cross was pinned to her left shoulder.

As the ride went along, I tried to move closer to the fascinating lady. Her face was full of peace and genuine caring for each person on the train. She chatted quietly with the person next to her and moved around the train, tending to people's needs as she saw them.

Suddenly, she sat down in the seat next to mine.

"What is your name?" she asked.

"I am Rosemary, a photographer. I was sent to catch a glimpse of the beauty and pain of India through photography. Who might you be?"

"I am Agnes Bojaxhiu, but you may know me as Mother Teresa."

"Are you kidding? Are you really Mother Teresa?"

"I am."

"Well, Mother. May I join you on your journey?"

"Do you love the poor? Will you help me care for the sick? Do you care about those who are weak? Will you care for the homeless, the lepers, and the blind? They are all God's children. If you are willing to assist me, you are welcome to come with me. If you take pictures, all I ask is that you respect the people and their feelings as you <u>record the images</u> for the world to see."

STORY QUESTIONS

1. What was Mother Teresa wearing?
   a. a white sari, with green trim, and a cross on her right shoulder
   b. a white sari, with blue trim, and a cross on both shoulders
   c. a white sari, with blue trim, and a cross on her left shoulder
   d. a blue sari, with blue trim, and a cross on her left shoulder

2. The author meets Mother Teresa . . .
   a. after searching for her.   c. in a restaurant.
   b. while taking photos in India.   d. on a train.

3. Who of these people did Mother Teresa **NOT** say she would help?
   a. the homeless   c. the blind
   b. the weak   d. the rich

4. "Record the images" probably means . . .
   a. take food to the hungry.   c. take pictures with a camera.
   b. write words in a journal.   d. photocopy people's passports.

DAILY Name _____ **Date** _____

Warm-Up 14

ROSA PARKS'S TALE

"Grandma, tell me the story again."

"Well, child, settle down and get cozy. The story is long and happened many years ago. It is a story about segregation, keeping people apart because of the color of their skin."

"Please tell me again."

"The shift at work had ended late, my feet were tired, and my mind was spent. Taking the bus home was the only way, because my husband and I did not have a car."

"Go on, Grandmother. What happened next?"

"At the bus stop, I waited for the right bus. When it arrived, I climbed on board and paid the driver the 25-cent fare to ride the bus. 'Colored folk in the back,' he said in a monotone voice."

"The back of the bus was crowded and full, but there were seats in the front of the bus that were still empty. <u>Confidently</u>, I walked to one of them and sat down."

"Go on, Grandmother."

"The bus screeched to a halt, and a policeman was called. He pulled me off the bus. Boy, was he mad! He was saying all kinds of stuff . . . words I don't even want to repeat."

"Please finish, Grandmother."

"Well, they took me to jail, charged me a $10.00 fine, and $4.00 for court. It wasn't too much fun sitting in that jail cell, but I had made my point. I was a citizen, just like the white folks. We all should be sittin' together."

"Grandmother?"

"Yes?"

"Did it do any good?"

"Yes, child. Today we walk down the same side of the street, go to the same restaurants, attend the same schools, and drink out of the same fountains. It was worth it."

STORY QUESTIONS

1. Who is listening to Rosa Parks tell the story?
   a. a granddaughter of Rosa Parks   c. the mother of Rosa Parks
   b. the grandfather of Rosa Parks   d. the neighbor of Rosa Parks

2. *Confidently* is a **synonym** for . . .
   a. boldly.   c. timidly.
   b. shyly.   d. quietly.

3. Why was Rosa Parks arrested?
   a. She was drinking from the wrong fountain.
   b. She sat in the white section of the bus.
   c. She sat in the colored section of the bus.
   d. She was waiting at the wrong bus stop.

4. What is one thing that Rosa Parks described that has changed since she got arrested?
   a. Today we all use the same type of telephone.   c. Today we all swim in the same pools.
   b. Today we all drink the same type of soda.   d. Today we all go to the same schools.

PRINCESS DIANA SHARES

Joe entered the shelter one stormy day on the outskirts of London. His clothes were wrinkled and soiled. He hadn't eaten in over three days, and his stomach was growling.

"Would you like a fresh bed and a shower?" a kind voice spoke to him.

In surprise, he looked up and gulped. There she was, the Princess of Wales, standing right there in this shelter. She was smiling at him.

Joe looked around. Maybe she was speaking to someone else. But no, he was the only one who had just come through the door.

He turned and gave her a grin. "Hey, Princess, are you speakin' to me?"

"I am," she said and returned his grin with one of her own.

Joe grabbed the towel and looked up. He saw a sign for the showers. He headed down the hall.

"Say, when I get myself all presentable, do you think I could ask you a few questions, Your Highness?"

Diana smiled again. "That would be just fine. Go ahead, get cleaned up. I'll have some hot soup waiting for you when you get out, and I'll show you to a bed. Looks like you could use a good night's sleep."

"I could! A warm bed would feel mighty nice. Thank you."

As Joe turned and headed into the showers, Diana thought, "This is why I came. If I can make the world a better place for just a few people, than I've accomplished my mission."

STORY QUESTIONS

1. Why did Joe call the volunteer "Princess"?
   a. because he was mean
   b. because he liked to tease
   c. because he recognized who she really was
   d. because he wanted to see if she would get mad

2. What important historical person was volunteering at the shelter?
   a. Prince Albert
   b. Princess Andrea
   c. Lady Sarah Spenser
   d. Princess Diana

3. In this passage, *soiled* most likely means . . .
   a. clean.
   b. dirty.
   c. new.
   d. happy.

4. Princess Diana was most likely a person who . . .
   a. didn't like people very much.
   b. didn't like living in the castle.
   c. liked to help people.
   d. always wore pretty dresses.

DAILY
Warm-Up 16
Name _____ **Date** _____

DOLLEY MADISON

"The White House is on fire!" yelled the servant from the kitchen area.

"Mrs. Madison, you must leave at once!"

Dolley turned around and watched as the kitchen burst into flames. The fresh biscuits for dinner were gone. The spaghetti, and soon the house, would go up in flames. As she glanced around, she realized that history would be lost, if she did not act quickly. She had to think fast.

Up the stairs she ran, grabbing the original oil painting of George Washington from the wall. It could not be redone. It could not be replaced.

Smoke billowed up the stairs.

"Madam," her servant cried. "Hurry! Run!"

Dolley nearly lost her footing at that very minute, but caught the banister. Smoke filled her nose, her eyes, and her mouth. She tried to breathe.

"Just get to the front door, and everything will be all right," she heard herself mutter. One foot in front of another . . . .

"Madam, where are you?"

"I'm here, Susanna."

"Follow the sound of my voice!"

Dolley followed the sound of her voice and soon reached the doors of the White House. Her lungs filled with air as she sprinted across the lawn with her coat flapping in the breeze. Her husband smiled as he saw her <u>hurry</u> across the lawn.

Under her arm was the precious painting of George Washington. Even in disaster, his amazing lady, Dolley, had saved a piece of history.

STORY QUESTIONS

1. Why was Dolley's servant telling her to leave the White House quickly?
   a. She had to go to the doctor.   c. A war had started.
   b. She was late for dinner.   d. It was on fire.

2. The opposite of *hurry* would be . . .
   a. breathe heavily.   c. move slowly.
   b. race.   d. move in circles.

3. What did Dolley do to save a piece of history?
   a. She took the painting of herself off the wall.
   b. She took the painting of Thomas Jefferson off the wall.
   c. She took the painting of George Washington off the wall.
   d. She took the painting of her husband off the wall.

4. Another name for this passage could be . . .
   a. "Oil Painting Escapes."   c. "Dolley's Worries."
   b. "Pretty as a Picture."   d. "The Lost Painting."

MATH MANIA

"What did you get on your test?" I reached over and grabbed Gary's paper. He reached over and grabbed it back.

He smiled weakly, and his answer was pathetic. "An F."

I grinned. "Beat ya! I got an A."

At recess my teacher, Ms. Lovell, asked me to stay in. Usually that wasn't a good sign. She said, "Travis, what do you think you could have done this morning instead of torturing Gary after the test?"

"Gee, Ms. Lovell, I guess I could have offered to help him, but he is just <u>awful</u> in math!"

"Well, Travis, sometimes you are aren't so good in other subjects, but you just happen to be a wizard at math. Why don't you trade time for the stuff you are good at, and he can help you with your writing? Will you just give it a try?"

"For how long?"

"There is another math project I'm assigning. I will give you a week to work on it. How does a week sound?"

"Okay."

After lunch, Ms. Lovell assigned us partners for the next math project. My partner was Gary, of course. We worked and worked—after school, before school, and on the weekend. When the project was due, we proudly presented it to the class. Gary knew what he was talking about, and I wrote a great report.

Then, the big surprise. Ms. Lovell gave us a pop quiz on the material! When she handed it back, Gary grabbed my paper. "Hey, Travis, what did you get?"

I stared in amazement. His paper had an A+ on it! Guess Ms. Lovell's idea had worked, a little too well! I moaned and grabbed my paper before he could see I only got an A.

STORY QUESTIONS

1. *Awful* is a **synonym** for the word . . .
   a. great.
   b. terrific.
   c. terrible.
   d. mad.

2. What did Ms. Lovell suggest to Travis?
   a. go home and study his writing and math facts
   b. swap time with Gary for things they were good at and help each other succeed
   c. get out on the playground and play hard
   d. swap time with Dillon and learn from each other

3. How was the experiment successful?
   a. The boys learned to fight better.
   b. The boys learned new ways to bug their teacher.
   c. The boys improved in areas that were their weakest.
   d. The boys learned how to cheat.

4. What do you think might happen next?
   a. Travis and Gary will continue to help each other and become friends.
   b. Travis and Gary will start cheating on their homework.
   c. Travis and Gary will give up and go back to bugging each other.
   d. Travis and Gary will get in a fight.

DAILY
Warm-Up 2

Name _____ Date _____

WRITE ON

"I hate writing!" wailed Anthony, as the substitute teacher entered the room. "It stinks, and I refuse to like it! Can't we do math instead?"

"Sorry," she said with a grin. "Your teacher says to work on writing, so writing it is."

The sub pulled a magnifying glass, a small notebook, and a trench coat out of her bag. We started to watch her intently. This didn't look like a normal lesson. What did this strange new sub with short, spiky hair have up her sleeve?

"How many of you have ever wanted to be a detective?" she asked. Everybody, even Anthony raised his hand.

"Well, being a good writer is just like being a good detective. You have to start with the right equipment. Cindy, what equipment would a good detective need to solve a mystery?"

"I think he would need to have a magnifying glass, a notebook, and a pen."

"That is a very good start! Tell me more . . . ."

As the class period moved along, we all became <u>absorbed</u> in the lesson. She reviewed things that were really important for successful writers. She talked about topic sentences, transition words, main ideas, details, and conclusions. At the same time, she kept going back to the detective equipment. It kept our attention, and before long we were coming up with great ideas and strong sentences. It was amazing! We were all feeling confident.

Bzzzz. The bell rang, signaling the end of the day. We were all caught by surprise. Where had the time gone? What spell had she cast over us so that we wanted to learn about writing? What if she was right, that writing was like being a detective? Could we really be successful writers, and like it too?

At that moment, Anthony <u>interrupted</u> my thoughts. "Hey, Miss A., do you think you could ask our teacher if you could come back another day? I think I might like to learn more about this writing stuff!"

I smirked to myself. If she had Anthony on her side, anything was possible.

STORY QUESTIONS

1. According to the passage, what equipment will help a detective?
   a. carrots, batteries, and a tape recorder
   b. camera, pen, and bottle of soda
   c. cars, boats, and planes
   d. magnifying glass, notebook, and pen

2. The opposite of *interrupted* is . . .
   a. bothering.
   b. not working.
   c. not bothering.
   d. unusable.

3. According to the passage, good writing includes . . .
   a. topic sentences, main ideas, details, transitions, and concluding sentences.
   b. topic sentences, main ideas, concluding sentences, and lots of adjectives.
   c. topic sentences, transitions, concluding sentences, and nouns.
   d. nouns, verbs, adjectives, and adverbs.

4. A **synonym** for *absorbed* could be . . .
   a. uninterested.
   b. bored.
   c. interested.
   d. happy.

DAILY
Warm-Up 3

Name _____ Date _____

SHOOT THE HOOPS

"Rebound, Alex!"

The ball bounced off the hoop, hitting Alex right on the top of the head. He crashed to the floor, and the crowd moaned.

Coach Winkler ran out onto the floor. Alex's breathing was very shallow. Coach motioned to the sidelines, and someone called for the paramedics.

Alex was our star player, and this was the championship game. We couldn't do it without him. Who else could rebound like Alex?

For several minutes we were all frozen as Alex lay stiffly on the floor. The ambulance arrived and put him on a stretcher. Our team was badly shaken, and the coach asked for a quick time out.

"Guys, this is the big game. I know you are all a bit shaken up about Alex. But he would want us to go out there, give it our best, and bring home that trophy. We have gotten this far as a team. I think we can give just a little more and do it for Alex."

We looked around. Everybody was sober, but we would give it our best shot.

The buzzer rang and we headed back to the floor. 2–2, 10–10, 20–21, the score continued to rise. We fought every basket and always managed to stay dead even with the other team.

At halftime, the score was tied again, 49–49. Coach Winkler gave us his best pep talk and informed us that Alex was cheering for us from his hospital bed. He had a concussion, but would be all right. In our <u>huddle</u>, we put our hands together in the middle and yelled as loudly as we could, "To Alex!"

The score continued to go back and forth. It would just be a matter of which team had the ball in the final seconds. Ten seconds to go. My team gave me the ball. As I dribbled down the court, I could hear Alex whispering in my ear, "Shoot from the center line. You can do it. We've practiced this forever." I aimed and shot the ball out of my hand. It went through the hoop like water rushing through a waterfall.

STORY QUESTIONS

1. *Huddle* is another way to say . . .
   a. group.
   b. school.
   c. family.
   d. basketball court.

2. What was the score at halftime?
   a. 2–2
   b. 10–10
   c. 49–49
   d. 21–21

3. Why was Alex on the basketball floor?
   a. He was too tired to move.
   b. Another player pushed him.
   c. He got hit in the head with the basketball.
   d. He didn't want to play in the game any more.

4. If you could make a prediction about the end of the game, it would most probably be . . .
   a. the team gets mad at Alex for quitting the game.
   b. Alex's team squeezes out a victory and wins the trophy.
   c. Alex's team loses by 10 points.
   d. all the players on the team cheat to win.

DAILY Warm-Up 4

Name _____ **Date** _____

ALL-STAR SOCCER

"Pass down the sideline," yelled Dad. He was our soccer coach for the All-Star team, Region 538.

Most of the time I liked having my dad as our coach, but today I wasn't in the mood. Our team was 17–0 and we were playing the championship game for our area. He kept yelling crazy stuff at me, and I just wanted him to be quiet. Why did he count on me to score so many goals?

I tried to concentrate, but I kept thinking back to last Friday after school. My sister and I had been fighting on the stairs. We banged into each other, and I peeled the skin all the way off my toe. It still hurt to wear my shoe, especially my soccer cleats. It even hurt to wear my sock. The sock stuck to my sore.

"J. D., go down the field! Take it in. Pass and control."

I glared at my dad, but I didn't want to tell him that I, fighting with my sister as usual, had torn all the skin off my right toe just before the championship game. I just wanted him to stop before I fell down holding my toe.

Suddenly, I heard a voice yell, "Hey J. D., guess that toe has you down!" It was my sister, Jill. She was so <u>annoying</u>. I'd show her.

The ball came right to me. I moved down the field, slicing, moving around the players. Fancy footwork. Left foot. Shoot and . . . .

"Oh, man! I missed the goal by an inch!"

"Good try, J. D.," yelled Dad. "Keep up the pressure."

I gritted my teeth and looked around the field for the ball. I saw my sister with an evil grin on her face. Time to buckle down and show her what I was made of!

STORY QUESTIONS

1. J. D. is having difficulty playing because . . .

　　a. she is thinking about her birthday party.　　c. she injured her toe.

　　b. she stayed up too late.　　d. she is feeling ill.

2. How did J. D. get injured?

　　a. She and her sister had been roughhousing on the stairs.

　　b. She had fallen when she was roller-blading.

　　c. Her sister bit her.

　　d. She had twisted her toe at soccer practice.

3. *Annoying* is a **synonym** for the word . . .

　　a. kind.　　c. bothersome.

　　b. smiling.　　d. handsome.

4. Another title for this passage could be . . .

　　a. "My Dad, The Coach."　　c. "I Love Soccer."

　　b. "Soccer Season."　　d. "The Troublesome Toe."

Name _____ Date _____

BASEBALL DAYS

Crack! The sound of the bat hitting the ball was almost as amazing as watching the ball sail out past third base. "Amazing hit, Seth!" yelled the coach. "Run like the wind!"

Seth rounded the bases as fast as he could. Just as he rounded third base, he didn't see the third baseman racing toward him. They collided as dust hit them both in the nostrils.

"Safe!" yelled the umpire.

Seth smirked at the third baseman. "Too bad, loser."

Whoosh! The baseman pushed him face first into the dirt.

Players ran on to the field. Players from both teams jumped in, slugging and punching.

Just at that moment, a swarm of bumblebees flew right into the center of the fight. They dove for the brightly-colored jerseys.

"Ouch! Hey! Help!"

All of the players scattered, running in all directions to escape the bees. The bees raced after them, getting closer and closer . . . .

"Seth. Seth! It's time to get up for school!"

"What? Huh? Hey, get off me! Stop stinging me!" Seth threw up his arms and accidentally hit his mom right in the nose. "Whoa! Sorry, Mom! I was having this crazy dream!"

"I could tell," said his mother, rubbing her nose.

STORY QUESTIONS

1. It turns out that Seth was . . .
    a. playing baseball.
    b. dreaming.
    c. rounding third base.
    d. eating waffles.

2. Why did the fight start at third base?
    a. The third baseman pushed Seth.
    b. Seth was looking for a fight.
    c. Seth called the baseman a loser.
    d. Seth and the baseman were enemies from school.

3. What brought the fight to a sudden end?
    a. bees
    b. the coach
    c. Seth's mother
    d. players from the other team

4. "Run like the wind" is a simile for . . .
    a. act like the wind.
    b. walk like the breeze.
    c. run in circles.
    d. run as fast as you can.

Name _____ Date _____

HARVEST FESTIVAL

It was the day of the annual fall festival, and each class was responsible for having a booth. There was a competition to see which booth brought in the most money for the fundraiser. The winner got a classroom pizza party.

Our fifth grade class had worked for weeks to plan our booth. Everyone pitched in, even Evan, the class clown.

We had voted to design a haunted house, not too scary, but not too babyish. All the kids had brought things from home, and some parents had even come on Friday night to help us set up after school.

I was the <u>president of operations</u>. It was my job to give the final okay before we opened for business.

As I surveyed our work, a smile crept over my face. Creepy black streamers, skeletons, and black lights hung from the ceiling. Large sheets of black plastic covered the floor, forming a path to walk through the maze. Dried leaves made crackly sounds as you walked down the path. Several students were hiding behind large, dark-colored objects to reach out and grab unsuspecting guests. A large, haunted house was hung on the wall. Soft lights shone through its windows, casting an <u>eerie</u> glow on the path.

Yes, we were ready for the carnival to begin. I gave my final approval to Melissa, my assistant. She flipped the switch, and the scary music began. The tour guides pulled up their Dracula hoods, and Alexis, the ticket taker, took her seat outside the door. The fun was about to begin.

STORY QUESTIONS

1. What does it mean to be "president of operations"?
a. to be the person everyone likes
b. to be the president of the United States
c. to be the person who runs classroom machines
d. to be in charge

2. Which is **NOT** something the class did to make the booth scary?
a. They sold tickets to the haunted house.
c. They played scary music in the booth.
b. They hung a haunted house on the wall.
d. They put dried leaves on the path to make crunching sounds.

3. A **synonym** for *eerie* could be . . .
a. spooky.
c. scared.
b. happy.
d. angry.

4. Why did the class want to have the best booth?
a. to scare the rest of the school
c. to win a class pizza party
b. to get free movie tickets
d. to get the most candy at Halloween

DAILY Name _____ Date _____
Warm-Up 7

BEACH DAYS

"Roller-blades in?"

"Check."

"Swimsuits and towels? Water bottles? Sandals? Extra change of clothes?"

"Check. Check. Check!" we yelled joyously.

"We're off!" said Dad, as he turned the key in the ignition.

We all put on our CD headphones and settled back for the ride. One and a half hours never goes slower than when you are headed to the beach for the day. We all just wanted to hurry up and get there. We all wanted to feel the sand between our toes, experience the wind in our hair, and the waves on our backs. We could taste the hot dogs and ice cream sandwiches at the small snack bar at the end of the roller-blading path. Skaters would be skating, kids would be building sandcastles, and people of all ages would be playing in the waves. Images poured through our minds as we bounced along in our minivan. We were all off in our own daydreams.

"Hey, guys, snap out of it. We're here."

"What? Dad, are you talking to us?"

"Hey, monkeys, we've been sitting in the parking lot for the past 10 minutes. Mom and I already have our blades on. Are you guys going to sit and daydream in the car, or are you going roller-blading with us?"

"We're on it!" we yelled in unison. In a flash, we were out of our seats. We ran for our skates and our cameras. Can't waste time when the beach is waiting!

STORY QUESTIONS

1. Where was the family headed for the day?
   a. to the beach
   b. to Hawaii
   c. on a bus tour
   d. to a park

2. What were the kids doing in the car when they arrived at the beach?
   a. crying
   b. singing
   c. daydreaming
   d. sleeping

3. According to this passage, which one is **NOT** a sight they would see at the beach?
   a. kids building sandcastles
   b. skaters on the roller-blading path
   c. mothers and fathers in bumper cars
   d. people playing in the waves

4. Another word for *joyously* is . . .
   a. sadly.
   b. happily.
   c. quickly.
   d. loudly.

DAILY Warm-Up 8

Name _____ Date _____

SKIING IN THE MOUNTAINS

My legs felt like rubber. My boots were pinching my feet and ankles. I didn't think I could go down one more hill. I wanted to just sit down and cry. I knew I had to continue, though. I was right in the middle of ski lessons on the top of the biggest hill at Snow Summit. Suddenly, the instructor stopped. "Chloe, are you all right?"

"I think so, but my boots hurt."

"Let me see if I can help," he said as he came over next to me. He checked the buckles, my socks, and the tightness of the boots.

"Ouch!" I screamed as he refitted the boot and snapped the bottom buckle in place. "That hurts!"

He unclipped the buckle, and we looked at my leg. There was a huge, blue bruise by my ankle. It was almost the size of a tennis ball.

"No wonder it hurts," he said. "You need to get these boots off, and get another pair. I don't think the rental boots are working for you."

"I don't think so, either," I <u>whispered</u>, as I examined the bruise that was getting more purple by the minute.

"Let's go down the hill and get these off. Then we'll talk to your dad. If you are going to keep skiing, you'll need boots all your own."

I gritted my teeth as I went down the slope. Boots all my own! No more rental boots, no more pain, no more bruises. That sounded mighty good to me!

STORY QUESTIONS

1. Why did Chloe get a bruise on her ankle?
   a. Her ankles were too small.
   b. Her skis were too big.
   c. Her rental boots didn't fit right.
   d. Her instructor didn't help her.

2. The opposite of *whispered* would be . . .
   a. spoke softly.
   b. in a soft voice.
   c. murmured.
   d. shouted.

3. How would you describe Chloe's mood at the beginning of the passage?
   a. tired and upset
   b. exhausted but happy
   c. eager and excited
   d. scared and angry

4. Another title for this passage could be . . .
   a. "Ski Boot Blues."
   b. "The Scariest Ski Slope Ever."
   c. "How I Broke My Leg Skiing."
   d. "I Hate Winter."

DAILY
Warm-Up 9

Name _____ Date _____

A DAY IN THE PARK

Swings move gently in the breeze. Silver slides shine in the sunlight. Monkey bars gleam with bright, colorful paint. Dew glistens on the grass. Birds chirp and fly to the picnic tables. Squirrels with mouths full of nuts dash through the grass. Lampposts blink off, done for the night. That's the park in the early morning hours.

In the middle of the day, mothers chatter and laugh with each other. Bright sunshine shimmers on the metal swings. Small birds sing loudly. Crows swoop down to pick up dropped crumbs. Children run and play, shrieking to each other. People lie on the grass, eating their picnic lunch. Grandmothers and grandfathers read books to toddlers. Parents cover their little ones with a blanket for a mid-afternoon nap.

The sun sets lower in the sky. Families start to pack up their belongings. The last few children gather their toys, bags, bikes, and skates. Mothers call their little ones' names, and fathers pack the cars. Animals start to settle in for the night. All is quiet.

Tomorrow is a new day and new adventures will be had.

STORY QUESTIONS

1. What time of the day is noisiest in the park?
   a. morning
   b. evening
   c. middle of the day
   d. middle of the night

2. Which one of these would you most likely see in the middle of the day?
   a. birds sleeping with their heads under their wings
   b. the moon overhead
   c. stars in the sky
   d. children pumping their legs on the swings

3. A **synonym** for *shimmers* could be . . .
   a. rains.
   c. dulls.
   b. shines.
   d. ruins.

4. What animals are **NOT** mentioned in the passage?
   a. dogs
   c. small birds
   b. squirrels
   d. crows

SAN FRANCISCO

"San Francisco is my favorite place to visit for several reasons," Jacob said aloud. He stood in the front of the classroom, giving his report.

"The city, first of all, has <u>amazing</u> sights to see. The Mission of San Francisco is a Catholic mission that was built right in the heart of the city. You can see fishing boats of all sizes parked at the pier, and seals making loud barking noises down by the docks. There is a museum, too, that has old games and machines from the past.

Many of the streets in San Francisco are very steep. One street, Lombard, is a tourist attraction. It zigzags back and forth from top to bottom. It is the most crooked street in the world!

San Francisco also has many different things you can do. Riding a cable car is exciting as you race up and down the narrow streets. There are many different types of restaurants to try. People can ride bikes, walk along the ocean, or roller-blade. Tourists can buy souvenirs or eat fresh clam chowder from bowls made of sourdough bread.

San Francisco is a place I could talk about for hours, but these are just a few reasons to go there for a visit."

"Wow!" said my teacher. "Wow, wow, wow! Let's just get in the car and go to San Francisco!"

We all cheered. Oh, if only we could.

STORY QUESTIONS

1. What was Jacob doing in class?
   a. singing a song
   b. giving a report
   c. acting in a play
   d. writing a report

2. *Amazing* is a **synonym** for the word . . .
   a. awful.
   b. horrid.
   c. incredible.
   d. nasty.

3. When Jacob's report came to an end, what did the class want to do?
   a. listen to more reports
   b. go to recess
   c. play math games
   d. take a trip to San Francisco

4. Which of the following is **NOT** an activity that Jacob mentioned?
   a. riding in a cable car
   b. watching a San Francisco Giants' baseball game
   c. eating clam chowder
   d. buying souvenirs

DAILY
Warm-Up 11

Name _____ Date _____

FACES IN SOUTH DAKOTA

As my dad flew the plane, my sisters and I all peered out the windows.

"What state are we over?" asked Jess.

"It's South Dakota."

"Isn't that where the monument is of the faces of four presidents?" asked Jen.

"You mean, Mount Rushmore, silly."

"Yeah, Mount Rushmore. Dad, will we fly by it?"

"We can, but we won't get too close. It's restricted air space. You might be able to use binoculars or capture it with Mom's telephoto lens."

"I want to use it!"

"Can't I use it, Mom? Please? I helped with the laundry before we left!"

"Tell you what. If you are speedy, you might each be able to snap a shot. I'll set the camera up, and you snap as fast as you can. Let's see if we all can hand it around."

Fortunately, Dad flew as close as he dared, and we handed the camera around from youngest to oldest.

When we got home, and developed the shots, we realized that we had each captured Thomas Jefferson, Abe Lincoln, Teddy Roosevelt, and George Washington from a slightly different angle.

"Great for all of us," said Amber, the oldest. "Our pages in our scrapbooks will all turn out differently. Thanks, Mom, for encouraging us all to take the shot."

STORY QUESTIONS

1. Which of the presidents below is **NOT** on Mount Rushmore?
- a. George Washington
- b. Thomas Jefferson
- c. Teddy Roosevelt
- d. Franklin Roosevelt

2. The monument, Mount Rushmore, is made up of . . .
- a. four presidents.
- b. four baseball heroes.
- c. four women.
- d. four famous teachers.

3. What do you think the girls' father does for a living?
- a. He is a tour guide.
- b. He is a stonecutter.
- c. He is a pilot.
- d. He is a baseball player.

4. What state was the family flying over?
- a. North Dakota
- b. South Dakota
- c. South Carolina
- d. South America

DAILY
Warm-Up 12

Name _____

Date _____

BAD HAIR DAY

Looking in the mirror, I groaned. The front of my hair was sticking up straight. Gel. That would fix it, I thought. But gel only made it worse. Hmmm. How about hairspray? No, that only made it sticky.

"Tyler, five minutes 'til we leave for school."

"Okay, Mom," I mumbled. "I just need some help on my hair."

"Did you try some gel?"

"Yes."

"Well, do the best you can. I'm putting your little sister in the car seat and then we have to leave. Okay?"

Suddenly, I had an idea. What if I put my head under water and used the hairdryer real quick? That was sure to help.

I dunked my head in the sink and came up dripping. Minutes later, with blow dryer in hand, the <u>image</u> in the mirror was not pretty. In fact, it was worse than the gel or hair spray. It was sticking up straight in all directions.

"Tyler, let's go, or you'll be late for school."

"Oh my gosh." My hair looked like a cyclone had hit it or maybe a tornado. What could I do?

As I headed for the door, I noticed my baseball cap. That was it. I grabbed it, pulled it on tight, almost to my ears, and headed out the door.

"No luck with your hair?" Mom said with a glint in her eye. "Why don't you start a new trend? You could call it 'The Tyler Tussled Look.'"

"Thanks a lot, Mom," I said as I slid into the car and fastened my seat belt. "I am sure it will be a big hit with all my friends." As Mom pulled up in front of the school, I opened the door to get out. As I was shutting it, Mom winked and said, "Good luck with your new trend."

STORY QUESTIONS

1. Which word would be a **synonym** for the word *image*?
   a. smile
   b. picture
   c. towels
   d. toothbrushes

2. What is Mom's name for a new hair trend?
   a. Tyler Time
   b. The Tyler Tussled Look
   c. Gel Boy
   d. The Funky Man

3. Which of these below didn't Tyler do to fix his hair?
   a. add gel
   b. add water
   c. use the hairdryer
   d. rewash his hair

4. What did Tyler finally do to fix his hair problem?
   a. He shaved his head.
   b. He combed his hair.
   c. He put on a baseball cap.
   d. He braided his hair.

DAILY Warm-Up 13

Name _____ Date _____

NO HOMEWORK

The day <u>droned</u> on and on. All my friends and I could think of was the movie we were going to see on the weekend and the party at Jake's.

Jake was the most popular boy in our class, and we were all camping out in his backyard in tents on Friday. No one was left out, and we all had our own ideas of what we could do to play pranks on each other.

My best prank was a secret that no one else knew about. I wasn't sure whom I would play it on yet, but it had to be done. I was so excited. The party was only two days away.

The birds outside the window got my attention. Two of them were fighting over a worm. I laughed, watching them.

Suddenly, Brandon jabbed me in the ribs. "Hey, you don't have any answers on your paper. What were you doing?"

"What? What?"

"Wise guy, we just took a pop quiz. You don't have any answers. The teacher said if we got an A on this pop quiz, we got to skip homework tonight. I don't know about you, but there are a lot of other things I'd rather do if I can have a night free of homework!"

I sighed and looked at my paper. Nothing. There was nothing there, not even my name. Quickly, I wrote a note to my teacher apologizing for not listening in class.

The facts were pure and simple. I had homework to do, and the choice had been mine. The lesson was tough, but it won't happen again next time. You can be sure of that!

STORY QUESTIONS

1. What words mean the same as *droned?*

    a. dragged on and on   c. left quickly

    b. ran away   d. went quickly

2. Which **compound word** means "an area behind your house"?

    a. weekend   c. backyard

    b. homework   d. outside

3. What is one thing that did **NOT** distract the author?

    a. thinking about a party on the weekend

    b. listening to the teacher

    c. thinking about playing a prank

    d. watching birds outside the window

4. What does it mean "to play a prank on someone"?

    a. to do nothing   c. to act like a monkey

    b. to do a trick or joke   d. to play your favorite CD

DAILY
Warm-Up 14

Name _____

Date _____

BEST FRIENDS

Julia and Vanessa have always been best friends for as far back as I can remember. They have been in the same class with the same teacher since kindergarten. They talk together on the phone, and they always play tetherball together at recess. They sit on the ramp before school and discuss all the boys, and they always sit together at lunch and share. Julia brings the drinks and sandwiches; Vanessa brings the snacks and fruit. Some days they switch, but they always share. Every Friday they wear matching shirts, and they always talk about going to Disneyland.

Today they were acting very unusual. Vanessa asked to sit with Cathy and me. Julia went off to play with Brittany and Brianna. It felt a little strange eating with Vanessa and not Julia.

No one said anything about it. We just ate our lunch and asked ourselves questions in our head. Why weren't they eating together? Why weren't they sharing lunch? Maybe we should investigate.

Cathy and I decided to talk to Vanessa, and Brittany and Brianna decided to talk to Julia.

Guess what we discovered? They just wanted to hang out with more friends because they had agreed that would be fun. We all liked the idea and planned to make a new group—a bigger group. It would be a group where we could all hang out, share our stuff, and talk about the boys on the ramp. I am looking forward to it.

STORY QUESTIONS

1. What happened at school that was unusual?
   a. Julia and Vanessa weren't eating together.
   b. Julia and Vanessa shared peanut butter sandwiches.
   c. Julia and Vanessa called each other.
   d. Julia and Vanessa went to Disneyland.

2. Which word in the passage means "to search or look for evidence"?
   a. plan
   c. share
   b. discover
   d. investigate

3. Where did the two girls talk about going all the time?
   a. Magic Mountain
   c. Disneyland
   b. Disney World
   d. the circus

4. How are things changing at the end of the story?
   a. The two girls ate lunch together, as usual.
   b. The two girls are finding out there are more nice people in their school.
   c. The two girls didn't learn anything.
   d. The two girls made a new club for themselves only.

Name _____ Date _____

EXCHANGE STUDENT

"I have the sign," said Lee. "I will hold it up. Kiri will know who we are because I have a sign." Lee was at the airport. Lee and her mother were picking up Kiri. Kiri was an exchange student. She was from New Zealand. She was going to stay with Lee and her family. She would stay for the summer.

Lee saw a girl come out of the gate. The girl smiled when she saw Lee's sign. She walked over to Lee. "Hi," said the girl. "I am Kiri. I am your exchange student. I have come to stay with you. I will learn about the United States. I will teach you about New Zealand. We will trade, or exchange, news. We will learn from each other."

Kiri saw how people in the United States lived. Both Lee and Kiri learned new things. Kiri learned the name of the national bird of the United States. The bird is the bald eagle. She liked the bald eagle's white head. Lee learned the name of the national bird of New Zealand. The bird is the kiwi. The kiwi cannot fly. It has a long bill. The bird's nostrils are on the tip of the bill! The kiwi lays only one egg. The egg is large. It is about one-third of the mother's weight!

Kiri and Lee learned how their countries are alike. Both of their countries have geysers. A geyser is a special spring. The spring shoots streams of boiling water and steam into the air. Only three countries have geysers. The United States has geysers. New Zealand has geysers. Iceland has geysers.

Lee learned that people called the Maoris settled New Zealand. They came long ago. They came in boats. Probably they came before 1,000 A.D.! Before the Maoris, all the mammals on New Zealand could fly! This was because the only mammals were bats! Non-flying mammals—like rats, cats, and sheep—came with people.

STORY QUESTIONS

1. When you exchange something, you . . .
- a. keep it.
- b. learn something about it.
- c. stay for a summer.
- d. trade it.

2. What is **NOT** true about the national bird of New Zealand?
- a. It is called the kiwi.
- b. It lays one egg.
- c. It can fly.
- d. It has nostrils at the tip of its nose.

3. This story is mainly about . . .
- a. birds.
- b. New Zealand.
- c. Lee and an exchange student.
- d. what Kiri learned.

4. How did mammals that cannot fly get to New Zealand?
- a. They swam to New Zealand.
- b. People brought them to New Zealand.
- c. They fell out of an airplane.
- d. The mammals grew there after people came.

Name _____   Date _____

MOVING DAY

The big, brown moving van sat in the driveway. Boxes were neatly packed in the back of the van. Everything we owned was in the back of that van. The car was full and so was Dad's truck. I was holding my favorite stuffed animal and my CD player.

Arnie, our German shepherd, was barking and racing around the yard. He knew something was different, but I don't think he really understood it was time to say goodbye to our old house, our friends, and everything we knew. Dad's job <u>transferred</u> him to Chicago, and now we all had to go along.

"Dad," I had moaned one night at the dinner table. "Why do we have to move? All my friends live here."

"I know, but you will make new friends. We will all have to make new friends."

"Cheer up. I think moving will be fun," Sarah, my older sister, said as she patted me on the head. "I can't wait to see the huge, new high school and meet bazillions of new friends."

I just hate when she pats me on the head. It makes me feel like a baby. I smiled weakly, and nodded my head. "All right, I'll give it a try. But if I don't like it, I am moving in with Dylan's parents. You'll see."

Now the big day was here. There was a knot in my stomach. I wanted to cry. My best friend Dylan came over to say goodbye. His parents had bought a big box of chocolates.

"These are to make you feel better on the road," whispered Dylan.

STORY QUESTIONS

1. Which word is **NOT** a synonym for *transferred?*
    a. relocated   c. moved
    b. flew   d. reassigned

2. How does Sarah feel about moving?
    a. She is excited.   c. She doesn't want to go.
    b. She has a knot in her stomach.   d. She thinks it will be horrible.

3. What does the author say he'll do if he doesn't like Chicago?
    a. He will run away.
    b. He'll move in with his friend Dylan's parents.
    c. He will move to California.
    d. He'll never go to school again.

4. What did Dylan and his parents bring to make everybody feel a little better?
    a. sandwiches for the drive   c. a box of chocolates
    b. gift certificates to the mall   d. a bag of cookies

DAILY
Warm-Up 17

Name _____ Date _____

SKI PANTS

Saturday morning dawned bright and sunny. Outside Kayla's window, the sun sparkled on the newly fallen snow. She jumped out of bed and reached for her clothes. Today was the first day to go skiing.

"Kayla, are you awake in there?" called her father.

She started to giggle. "That's a foolish question. Of course, I'm awake! I have no intention of sleeping in today!"

As Kayla came down to breakfast, her father was sitting at the table doing his morning crossword puzzle. Her mom was spreading strawberry jam on her toast, and her brother was stuffing doughnuts into his mouth until his cheeks <u>puffed out like a chipmunk</u>.

"Hey, leave some for me!" she screeched as she entered the kitchen.

Dad looked up. "My goodness. It looks as if you have outgrown your ski pants. They're a few inches too short on you."

"They'll be just fine," muttered Kayla as she reached across the table to grab the last chocolate donut.

Rrrrrip! Everyone looked up in surprise. Kayla's pants had split right down the seams from top to bottom.

"Looks like we need to head to the store before we head to the slopes," whispered Mom with a grin.

Even Kayla had to let out a giggle. "Guess you're right. I guess I have grown."

STORY QUESTIONS

1. What does the phrase "puffed out like a chipmunk" mean in the passage?
   a. His cheeks were bulging with doughnuts.　　c. He was taking pictures of chipmunks.
   b. He was turning into a chipmunk.　　d. He was practicing for the school play.

2. Why did Kayla giggle when her dad asked if she was awake early?
   a. She loved his jokes in the morning.
   b. She thought his voice sounded funny.
   c. She didn't giggle.
   d. She was too excited about skiing to sleep late.

3. Which breakfast word is spelled correctly in two different ways in this passage?
   a. strawberry　　c. chocolate
   b. doughnut　　d. toast

4. What **compound word** describes what Kayla had done with her snow pants?
   a. ingrown　　c. everyone
   b. outgrown　　d. strawberry

Name _____   **Date** _____

RAY'S SMIRK

Bob threw his backpack under the coat rack and headed into the classroom. He was late to school, again. He just hated being late, but his little brother always forgot something, dropped something, or forgot to brush his teeth.

"Go to the office and get a tardy slip," said Mr. Forest flatly.

Bob turned to leave. Suddenly, he noticed Ray coming out of the coatroom with a big smirk on his face. He wondered what he might be up to.

During the morning, Bob looked over at Ray. He was still wearing that silly smirk. He had to be up to something.

Lunchtime came and went. Mr. Forest <u>rambled</u> on about blizzards, flower blossoms, and Bob still wondered what Ray had up his sleeve.

As they left school, Ray gave Bob that same silly look, one more time. Bob said, "What?"

"You'll find out soon enough, late guy!"

When Bob got home, he reached into his backpack to get out his homework. His hand hit something soggy. He reached in again and then groaned. What was all over his backpack? Bob grabbed his flashlight and prepared for the worst.

"Yuck! My backpack is full of already chewed bubble gum! Yuck! Yuck! Yuck!"

STORY QUESTIONS

1. Which word or words mean the same as *rambled*?

    a. walked   c. stopped

    b. talked on and on   d. woke up

2. What trick did Ray play on Bob?

    a. He told the teacher Bob cheated.   c. He put gum in Bob's backpack.

    b. He put ants in Bob's lunch box.   d. He put candy in Bob's pocket.

3. Why was Bob worried all day?

    a. He didn't know what to do about coming to school late.

    b. He didn't know why Ray was giving him funny looks.

    c. He was hungry and wanted lunch.

    d. He thought Mr. Forest would give him extra homework.

4. What could be an **antonym** for *smirk*?

    a. smile   c. laugh

    b. grin   d. frown

DAILY Name _____ Date _____
Warm-Up 2

MISSING KEY

"Don't forget to take the key to school with you today, Nolan. Remember it's the day I stay late at work."

"Okay, Dad," I said. "I will put it in a safe place."

Dad and I lived alone in a two-bedroom apartment. He had to work late on Wednesday nights, so I always had to let myself in and eat leftovers for dinner. Mrs. Robbins, the neighbor, always kept an eye on me so Dad didn't have to worry. She loved it if I came to visit, and she would even feed me snacks. Her kitchen always smelled of fresh cookies, so I didn't mind too much.

As I left for school, I placed the key in the usual spot, under the plant by the door. I then headed down the street to school.

Christian, the class bully, was waiting for me at the corner for the morning torture time. "Headed to school are you, daddy's boy?"

I just wanted to haul off and hit him, but Dad said violence never solved a thing. "Just keep walking," I told myself.

Christian <u>taunted</u> me for a few more minutes, and finally left me alone. It was useless to talk back. He would just keep being his regular bully self.

After school, I cut across the vacant lot so I would avoid getting tortured. Usually, it took about 10 minutes to get home. Today, it took five. My breathing was short, and I just wanted to get in the house. "Quick, get the key, and get in the house," I thought.

I reached for the key under the plant. It was gone . . .

STORY QUESTIONS

1. Why did Nolan have to remember the house key?
   a. so he could let himself in when Dad worked late
   b. so he could go home any time during the day
   c. so he could have friends over
   d. so he could take his dad to lunch

2. Nolan didn't mind visiting with Mrs. Robbins because . . .
   a. she grew flowers and plants in her garden.
   b. she wouldn't talk to him.
   c. she wrote letters to her children.
   d. she made him cookies.

3. A **synonym** for the word *taunted* could be . . .
   a. laughed.   c. smiled.
   b. teased.   d. helped.

4. Why didn't Nolan hit Christian?
   a. He knew Christian could hurt him if he tried.
   b. His dad told him violence never solves anything.
   c. He didn't want to get in trouble at school.
   d. He wanted to wait until he found a friend who could help him.

DAILY Warm-Up 3

Name _____ Date _____

MOVING LIGHT

"Whatever are we looking for?" whispered my friend, Celine, as we sat by the window in my dark bedroom.

"It's a light that moves across the vacant lot whenever it is dark at night," I whispered back.

"How many times have you seen it?"

"Every night for the past three days. It usually starts about 10 o'clock and moves around for about 30 minutes."

"Do you think someone is trying to hide a dead body?"

"I don't know. It was giving me the willies. That's why I asked you to watch with me."

"Did you tell your parents?"

"No. I thought I would have you watch to make sure I wasn't imagining things before I told them."

We watched silently. At 10 P.M. sharp, a small light moved across the vacant lot. It bobbed and twisted. It stopped moving and then started again. We both gasped. A motor started making a loud angry sound. We began to shriek.

Suddenly, my mom arrived at our bedroom door. "Girls, are you okay?"

"We're not sure, Mom. There is a light that is moving in the vacant lot across the street."

Mom came over and watched. "It does look suspicious. Maybe we should call the police."

STORY QUESTIONS

1. Which word do you think is **NOT** a synonym for *willies*?
   a. chills
   b. creeps
   c. giggles
   d. jitters

2. Mom thought it would be best to . . .
   a. huddle together and have a group hug.
   b. go to the vacant lot and explore.
   c. make hot chocolate and cookies.
   d. call the police.

3. Why was Celine staying overnight?
   a. They were celebrating her birthday.
   b. Her friend was scared to watch out her window alone.
   c. They were going to the mountains in the morning to snowboard.
   d. Celine was scared of the dark.

4. If a lot is *vacant*, that means that it is . . .
   a. empty.
   b. full.
   c. beautiful.
   d. ugly.

DAILY
Warm-Up 4

Name _____ Date _____

ABANDONED BUS

"Hey, look at this!" my friend, Cindy, yelped. "It's an abandoned bus."

Frannie and I stopped and stared. We were speechless. Right in front of us, hidden in the thick bushes, was a bus—an old broken-down school bus.

"Let's go inside," Frannie said.

"No way! It isn't ours. Besides, someone might be living in there."

"That would be hard to believe," whispered Cindy. "The trees are grown all around the bus. You can't even see the windows." We walked all around the bus, but the windows were boarded up or covered with thick branches from the trees. Moss was growing on the bumper, and the license plate was covered in mud.

Suddenly, we heard the <u>crackling</u> of twigs breaking as footsteps approached. We ducked, jumping behind a large oak tree. None of us dared to breathe.

A tall, thin man wearing a black trench coat and dark glasses was coming down the path. He had a magnifying glass in his hand, and he was carrying a briefcase. He had a thick mustache and bushy eyebrows.

Without warning, as if he had pressed a magic button, the door of the bus opened, and the man disappeared inside.

Cindy, Frannie, and I all looked at each other. We tiptoed around to the back of the bus and tried to peer in the windows.

"Give me a lift," whispered Frannie softly.

As she looked in the window, she let out a low whistle. "Would you look at that!"

STORY QUESTIONS

1. What do you think the girls were doing when they discovered the bus?
   a. reading
   b. exploring
   c. writing stories
   d. figuring out math problems

2. Which of the following is a **synonym** for *crackling*?
   a. blaring
   b. hissing
   c. crunching
   d. booming

3. Why was it difficult to see inside the bus?
   a. The windows were closed and there were curtains that were shut.
   b. It was guarded by a dog.
   c. The windows were boarded up or covered with thick branches.
   d. The windows had been painted over with black paint.

4. Which of the following is **NOT** part of the description of the man in the passage?
   a. He has a bright smile.
   b. He was holding a magnifying glass.
   c. He has bushy eyebrows.
   d. He has a thick mustache.

DAILY Name _____ Date _____
Warm-Up 5

CHOCOLATE SNAPSHOT

In the summertime, when things get boring, my friends Hank, Victor, and I often ride our bikes to the edge of town and go exploring.

Today started out as just a regular day. We had already swum in Victor's pool, played cards in Hank's garage, and shot off a rocket in my backyard.

"Let's head out to the edge of town," exclaimed Hank.

"If we pack a lunch, we can explore the hayloft at the old barn, dabble with fishing at the stream, or ride to the old broken-down castle that is way out of town."

"The castle!" Victor and I said <u>in unison</u>.

"I'll bring chocolate milk, celery, and cheese!"

"I've got the sodas, sandwiches, and chips!"

"I guess that means I bring the camera," said Hank.

Within ten minutes we were off, riding down the road on our bicycles at <u>breakneck speed</u>. We rounded the corner in front of the old castle so fast that the basket went flying off the front of Victor's bike.

"Great time for a snapshot!" yelled Hank.

We all laughed as he grabbed his camera.

The cheese, celery, and chocolate milk lay scattered on the ground in a big syrupy mess.

"Say cheese!" Victor and I smiled. "Who knows what adventures await us in the castle?"

STORY QUESTIONS

1. Why did the boys want to go exploring?
   a. They wanted to try out their new bikes.
   b. They wanted to see the new town.
   c. They were already bored.
   d. They loved riding in the rain.

2. The words "in unison" means . . .
   a. together, at one time
   b. separately, all alone
   c. in a group, with only one leader
   d. in groups of two or three

3. Another way to say "breakneck speed" would be . . .
   a. moving extremely slow.
   b. moving extremely fast.
   c. moving to the beat.
   d. moving to another town.

4. Which of the following is **NOT** an activity the boys had already done that day?
   a. swimming in Victor's pool
   b. playing cards in Hank's garage
   c. shooting a rocket off in the backyard
   d. riding their bikes to the movies

DAILY
Warm-Up 6

Name _____

Date _____

MISSING DOG

"Hey, Dad. Look at this." We were standing next to the mailboxes. A large sign was posted on them. It read: Missing Dog. Answers to the name of Ginger. Cocker spaniel, tan with markings. Collar around her neck. If found, call 868-2902.

"Doesn't that sound like the dog we saw running down the street this morning?"

"It surely does. Let's keep our eyes peeled as we drive home. We might see her again."

We looked and looked as we drove home, but there was no sign of Ginger. I begged Dad to drive around the neighborhood one more time.

"We just might see her, if we go around one more time."

"Okay," he said. "We have time, so let's give it a whirl."

I opened my window to call her name. "Ginger. Ginger. Here girl."

Dad continued to drive down the street. Finding Ginger seemed <u>impossible</u>.

"Dad, watch out!" A tiny blue car with a pizza sign on top cut us off as we were about to turn left into our street. Right as we swerved to miss the car, I noticed a flash of tan and white in the car's mirror.

"Stop!" I wailed. I jumped out of the car and ran behind it.

Right there in the middle of the road was a little dog that looked just like the poster. She was whimpering, but I managed to pick her up. I struggled back to the car.

Dad and I drove back to the mailboxes and got the number to call. Dad let me dial it.

"Hello," a sad voice answered the phone.

"Hello," I said. "I think I have a surprise for you!"

STORY QUESTIONS

1. Where did the boy find out about the missing dog?
   a. from a sign on the mailboxes
   b. from a billboard on the mailboxes
   c. from a sign on the freeway
   d. from an ad in the newspaper

2. Which of these does not mean *impossible*?
   a. without a solution
   b. unworkable
   c. achievable
   d. not possible

3. Which of the following is part of the description of the dog?
   a. black with stripes
   b. tan with markings
   c. brown with spots
   d. small with a long tail

4. What do you think the boy and his dad will do next?
   a They will try to find the pizza driver.
   b. They will return the dog to her owner.
   c. They will keep the dog and name her Fluff.
   d. They will take the dog to the vet.

Name _____ Date _____

CALLED FOR CHEATING

After the game was over, we all headed toward the locker room, cheering loudly. Our team had just won the first game of the football season, with the final score being 21–17.

Suddenly, I felt a push from behind. I turned around and saw it was the quarterback from the other team. He was glaring at me. "I've got a bone to pick with you!" he said.

My teammates and I felt instantly uncomfortable. They started to hurry to the locker room, leaving me alone with the bully from the other team.

"Hey!" he said. "I saw you trip my teammate and hold him back when the referee wasn't watching."

I just stood there. I didn't deny it. I had tripped the guy, but it really wasn't on purpose. "Look," I said. "I didn't mean to. It just happened. When I turned around, he was right there, and I bumped into him. We both tripped. Don't you remember?"

"Yeah, right!"

"I'm serious. It was an accident."

Just at that moment, Coach Bentley stepped out the door of the locker room. "Brain!" he yelled. "Get yourself in here and get out of that uniform. We have some tape to watch, and you have to see it."

The quarterback sneered at me and said, "I guess you get off this time, but I'll be back." He turned and walked toward the bus where the rest of his team was waiting. As I turned back and headed to the locker room I muttered, "Saved by the coach!"

STORY QUESTIONS

1. Which of the following means the same as *sneer*?
   a. sweet smile   c. cruel smile
   b. funny grin   d. sad frown

2. "I've got a bone to pick with you" means . . .
   a. I want to talk to you.
   b. I want to share a wishbone with you.
   c. I want to look at a skeleton for Halloween.
   d. I am choking on a chicken bone.

3. What did the quarterback accuse the other player of doing?
   a. scoring a touchdown illegally
   b. making faces at the referee behind his back
   c. purposely tripping a player from the other team
   d. running out of bounds

4. What nickname did the coach yell to the player?
   a. Buddy   c. Brian
   b. Bobby   d. Brain

A HAUNTED HOUSE?

The rain was pounding on the roof as I tried to sleep. It sounded like a downpour. We had just moved into our new house. It wasn't really new, but it seemed new to us. Our old house was too small since Mom had the baby, so we had bought a new house right up the street. Our address had changed from 123 Sycamore to 137 Sycamore.

The problem was that all the neighbors said the new house was haunted. All my friends teased me when they found out we were moving. I just let their words go <u>in one ear and out the other</u>.

Suddenly, I sat straight up in bed. Something was moving outside my window. Lying back down, my mind started to imagine things. Shadows moved across my wall, lightning flashed outside the window. Suddenly, a light shone on my window and my nightlight flickered and went out.

Several minutes later, a moaning sound came from outside my door. I jumped out of bed, put my feet into my warm, fuzzy slippers, and grabbed my baseball bat. Whatever it was, it was not going to frighten me again.

I reached for the door handle and started to open it.

"Boo!" yelled my big brother Alfred. He was standing in the hall with a long stick with a lantern on the end. He was wearing dark glasses and a long, black rain jacket.

"Did I scare you?" he asked.

I stood up to my full height. "No, of course not. I was just going to the kitchen to get a glass of water!"

We both burst into fits of laughter and rolled on the carpet in the hallway of our new house.

STORY QUESTIONS

1. "In one ear and out the other" is a idiom meaning . . .
   a. not really pay attention to what's being said.
   b. use a cotton swab to clean your ears.
   c. put things in one ear and pull it out the other.
   d. put something in and pull it out.

2. Why did the kids at school tease the person telling the story?
   a. They knew the previous owner, and he was creepy.
   b. They were scared of the big windows in the new house.
   c. They were jealous that their parents hadn't bought the house.
   d. They said the new house was haunted.

3. Why did the family move?
   a. The old house was too big since one brother moved away.
   b. The old house was too small since the grandparents came to live with them.
   c. The old house was too small once the mom had another baby.
   d. The old house was haunted.

4. Who was behind the scary noises?
   a. the father
   b. the big sister
   c. the big brother
   d. the next-door neighbor

DAILY Warm-Up 9 Name _____ Date _____

SECRET CODE

"This code is so hard," moaned Jacob. "Do you have the paper that tells me how to crack it?"

"I forgot where I put it," said Justin. "I didn't write it, you know."

"You didn't? Who did? I thought we were the only two who had this code," said Jacob.

"Don't know. Guess this adds to the mystery."

Justin and Jacob went in to the classroom. Justin checked his desk, his backpack, and in his cubby. The secret code was nowhere to be found. As he looked again, there was another note in his cubby, written in code.

"What! Who has our secret code? I think someone has stolen it from us."

"Hey, Justin, what are you looking for?" smirked Savannah as she sneaked up behind him. "It wouldn't be something secret, would it?"

Justin's head jerked up, and he looked her square in the eye. "What did you say?"

"I said, I was wondering if you lost something important. You seem <u>frustrated</u> and frantic. Am I right?"

"What's it to you?"

"Well, Samantha and I have been thinking. If you two let us in on your secret stuff, we might be able to help you find what you're missing."

Both boys looked at her. "Guess you two have our top secret information."

"We do," she sneered. "And if you want it back, you have to let us into your club."

The boys exchanged looks. What harm could it do?

STORY QUESTIONS

1. What do you think is something the boys really like to do?
   a. do math problems and compare answers   c. write in secret code
   b. read mystery stories and talk about them   d. play pranks on the girls

2. When Jacob wants to "crack" the code it means . . .
   a. he wants to crack it open on the desk.
   b. he wants to solve it.
   c. he wants to open it using a nutcracker.
   d. he wants to smash it.

3. A **synonym** for *frustrated* could be . . .
   a. irritated.   c. happy.
   b. pleased.   d. excited.

4. How did the girls get the boys' attention?
   a. by telling the teacher about the code
   b. by hiding in the classroom
   c. by stealing their code
   d. by talking to them at recess

DAILY
Warm-Up 10

Name _____ Date _____

LETTERS IN THE MAIL

"This year I'm <u>turning over a new leaf</u>," said Matilda. "From now on I am going to write to Grandma Beanie every week."

The first week, she wrote her letter and mailed it off. Matilda <u>filled</u> it with riddles and fun jokes. Grandma Beanie sent back a letter full of more riddles and jokes.

The second week, she sent Grandma Beanie a beautiful picture of the beach and a story she had written at school. Grandma Beanie sent her a picture or herself as a child on the beach and a story she had written.

Each week, Matilda tried to send different types of things to Grandma, and Grandma always sent back the same type of things.

One day, she asked, "Mom, what could I send Grandma Beanie that would be very unusual?"

"Why don't you send her a puzzle and your school picture this year?"

"What a great idea!" The week before Thanksgiving, Matilda sent Grandma Beanie a puzzle and a picture of herself at age 9. However, she did not realize that several pieces of the puzzle fell under her bed when she slipped it into the envelope. Matilda licked the envelope, sealed it, and stuffed it in the mailbox.

The next week, she got the surprise of her life. When she came home from school, there were three letters waiting for her. Each one was from Grandma Beanie. Each envelope had 10 puzzle pieces inside. None of them fit together into a complete puzzle.

"What's this all about?" she wondered. Matilda ran to the phone and called Grandma Beanie.

"My dear," said Grandma. "Some of the pieces are missing from my puzzle, so I decided to play a trick on you. Each day you get three envelopes. Each envelope has 10 pieces. At the end of 10 days, put the puzzle together and see what you have!"

STORY QUESTIONS

1. What does it mean when Matilda uses the idiom "turning over a new leaf"?
   a. She's going to the garden to collect leaves.
   b. She's going to turn around and around many times.
   c. She's going to make a fresh start and do better than before.
   d. She is going to use leaves in a new art project.

2. An **antonym** for *filled* could be . . .
   a. crammed.
   b. overflowing.
   c. empty.
   d. jam-packed.

3. Why did the puzzle Grandma got in the mail have pieces missing?
   a. Matilda was playing a joke on her grandmother.
   b. Matilda had dropped some under her bed.
   c. Matilda was getting even with her grandmother.
   d. Matilda wanted her grandmother to guess what the other pieces were.

4. What do you think will be on the puzzle when Matilda gets all of the pieces?
   a. a picture of the ocean waves
   b. a picture of Grandma when she was 9 years old
   c. a picture of Hawaii
   d. a picture of a dog and cat

Name _____   Date _____

SOCKS

"Roll out, girls!" yelled our camp counselor. "It's time to rise and shine."

All ten of us in the cabin moaned and pulled the sleeping bags over our heads. "Just let us sleep for 10 more minutes. PLEASE!"

"No way. Time to get up and clean this cabin. Today is the day for the big sock race, and we are going to win!"

Avery, Jenna, and Kelly rolled off their bunks. Thud! I rolled off the top bunk and hit the floor. "Help! I'm being attacked by a giant sock!"

"I think you mean a sleeping bag!" laughed Kelly.

We ran outside and gathered under the flagpole.

"Today is the big day," stated the head counselor. "It is the day for the longest sock race. When I blow the whistle, each counselor will come and pick up a bag. Each team will have socks in the bag. Tie all the socks together until the timer goes off. The team with the longest string of socks wins!"

"We're gonna win! We're gonna win!" we all screamed at once.

The whistle blew, and our counselor ran to get a sack of socks. She picked a blue travel bag and ran back to our line.

"Quickly!" she screamed. "Get the socks out and start tying!"

Avery opened the bag. Somberly, she said, "There's a note. It says, 'Dear counselor, we ran out of socks. If you want to win, solve the problem on your own!'"

"Oh, my gosh!"

"Oh, no!"

"Back to the cabin for socks!" we yelled, and off we <u>galloped</u>.

STORY QUESTIONS

1. How can the campers win the race?
   a. by creating the longest chain of socks
   b. by taping socks to the trees
   c. by collecting dirty socks in the biggest pile
   d. by putting the socks in the largest washer

2. When the girls "galloped" off to the cabin, it means . . .
   a. galloped like horses.   c. ran very fast.
   b. jumped on horses and rode them to the cabin.   d. skipped.

3. The campers are going to solve the problem of the empty bag by . . .
   a. using their own socks.
   b. stealing socks from other cabins.
   c. calling their parents to bring them fresh socks from home.
   d. running to the store and buying more socks.

4. What would be a good ending for this story?
   a. Even though they had an empty bag, the girls filled it with dirty laundry.
   b. Even though their counselor was kind, the girls never finished before the bell.
   c. Even though the socks were dirty, they were still able to get them clean.
   d. Even though they had sock problems, the girls were able to win the contest of the socks.

DAILY
Warm-Up 12

Name _____ Date _____

CYCLONE IN THE HOUSE

This past week I went to stay with my grandma and grandpa. I always go there for a week in the summer. They live on a farm. There isn't much time for television at their farm, but I don't care because we have so much to do. I get to help Grandpa milk the cows, and help Grandma collect eggs from the chickens. She shows me how to steal the eggs carefully when the hens aren't looking. Grandpa teaches me not to mistake melons for onions in the garden and how to dig for carrots and radishes.

When I got home from the farm, I was ready to plop down on my bed and take a long rest. I was ready to watch movies, chat with friends, and play video games with my sister.

Grandpa brought me home and dropped me off outside the door. He had waved goodbye and drove off without coming in. He was running late for his dentist appointment. When I walked in the house, it looked like a cyclone had hit it. Towels were hanging on the backs of chairs, juice was all over the kitchen table, and mud was caked on the floor. I wrinkled my nose in <u>disgust</u>. Where was my mom? What had happened to our house?

I walked down the hall in a daze. Mom had made sure when I left for Grandma's and Grandpa's that I left my room neat as a pin. Opening the door to my room, I gasped in horror. Dirty socks were on the floor. The books were all out of the bookshelf. Broken toys littered the room. What was going on?

I shut my eyes tight. I tried to collect my thoughts. When I opened them, I scanned the room again, then glanced up and down the hallway. I knew what was wrong.

Sprinting for the door with my duffel bag in my hand, I ran out the front door. All the houses on our street look the same. I was in the neighbor's house!

STORY QUESTIONS

1. Which of these didn't the person in the story do at Grandma's?
   a. milk cows
   b. cook omelets
   c. dig for carrots
   d. collect eggs

2. This passage is written in . . .
   a. third person.
   b. second person.
   c. first person.
   d. fourth person.

3. Which word is a **synonym** you could use for the word *disgust* in the passage?
   a. loathing
   b. entertainment
   c. enjoyment
   d. happiness

4. What mistake did Grandpa make?
   a. He dropped his grandchild off at the wrong house.
   b. He went to the wrong dentist.
   c. He forgot to brush his teeth first thing in the morning.
   d. He was driving the wrong car.

JELLY BEAN PLANET

The rain was coming down heavily as I stood on the balcony of our apartment. It rained every day on our planet. Whenever I walked in the rain, I just opened my mouth to taste blueberry, raspberry, or a touch of licorice. The rain was delicious.

Running back inside to get out of the rain, I flopped onto the couch. It smelled of strawberries and cream. The pillow smelled like orange marmalade. Everywhere I walked, everything I did, fruity smells reached my nose.

I looked at the buildings outside our windows. There were tall blue ones, short green ones, and yellow oval ones as far as the eye could see. Some of the buildings had crazy patterns of several colors swirled on the sides. Fruity colors were everywhere.

"Breakfast, Son," my dad called. "It's jelly beans on toast and pancakes with jelly bean syrup."

"Awesome!" I <u>bellowed</u> from upstairs. "I'll be right there!"

Bounding down the stairs, I heard Mom calling, "Would you like a peanut butter sandwich with blackberry jelly beans or one with cherry?"

"Cherry," I called. "By the way, Mom, could you throw in the chocolate jelly bean cake for lunch?"

"Sure," she added.

"This is delicious!" exclaimed Dad. "The only thing wrong with this planet is the dentist bill every month!"

STORY QUESTIONS

1. Why was everything sweet on this planet?
a. It was the land of pie.
b. It was only sweet on the weekdays.
c. It was made of jelly beans.
d. There was too much chocolate.

2. A **synonym** for *bellowed* could be . . .
a. shouted.   c. said.
b. whispered.   d. guessed.

3. Which profession do you think would make a lot of money on this planet?
a. photographer   c. librarian
b. dentist   d. taxi driver

4. Which of the following was **NOT** one of the foods mentioned in the passage?
a. pancakes with jelly bean syrup   c. bacon with jelly bean sauce
b. chocolate jelly bean cake   d. jelly beans on toast

DAILY
Warm-Up 2

Name _____   Date _____

MY DAY AS A PANCAKE

Mallory rolled out of bed on the morning of the first day of school. She was feeling excited. Her new school outfit hung in her closet; the new shoes were by the door. Her fancy hair ribbons were sitting on her desk.

The sight that greeted her eyes in the mirror horrified her. She blinked and looked a second time.

"Mom!" she called. "Please come here immediately!"

"Just a moment, honey. I'm frying the bacon."

"Mom, it's an emergency!"

"What could be such an emergency this morning?" asked Mom as she climbed up the stairs. Suddenly, she stopped. "Mallory, is that you under there?"

"Yes, Mom, it's me. Something must have happened in the middle of the night! Do I look like a puffy pancake to you?"

"What did you eat? Did you drink something unusual?"

"Well, I did drink a chocolate shake that a stranger at the store gave me yesterday."

"Mallory, you know what we've said about taking things from strangers!"

"I know, Mom, but what can we do about it now? I've already turned into a pancake, and I don't know how to change back. What am I going to do? It's the first day of school!"

Mallory tried to get out of her pajamas but could barely <u>wiggle</u> her toes. She was stuck. Her mom called the doctor, and she said to come immediately.

"So much for wearing my new outfit and my new shoes," grumbled Mallory. She had been so excited about the first day of school. Now, though, she was glad that she didn't have to go to school looking the way she did. No matter how fantastic her clothes were, they couldn't hide the way she looked today!

STORY QUESTIONS

1. What discovery did Mallory make when she got out of bed?
   a. Her new outfit for school didn't fit.
   b. She had become an apple.
   c. She had become a pancake.
   d. A stranger was sitting in her room.

2. A **synonym** for the word *wiggle* would be . . .
   a. touch.   b. take off.   c. move.   d. sit.

3. What unwise choice had Mallory made the day before?
   a. She had crossed the street without looking both ways.
   b. She didn't brush her teeth before bed.
   c. She had taken something from a stranger.
   d. She hadn't put on her seatbelt.

4. Why didn't Mallory put on her new clothes for school?
   a. She was stuck in her pajamas and couldn't get them off.
   b. She didn't like the new clothes and didn't want to put them on.
   c. She was hungry and she wanted to eat breakfast first.
   d. She had gotten them dirty the day before.

DAILY Warm-Up 3   Name _____   Date _____

LIFE OF A FLOWER

Poppy Flower was born in a large flower patch on the edge of the town of Rose View. Her parents were Daisy and Sweet William.

From the moment she was born, she <u>grew like a weed</u>. She grew to her full height very fast. Her leaves were vibrant green, and her petals were the brightest shade of orange anyone had ever seen.

Before long, all her friends started calling her "Fireball" because her colors were so bright.

Poppy often spent her days painting and was brilliant with an artist's paintbrush. Poppy painted picture after picture, selling them to galleries across the nation.

By the time she was four, she had been featured in *Flower Power* and *Flower Time* magazines. All the magazines wanted to do articles on her, even the gossip magazines. Photographers followed her everywhere.

Although Poppy was tired of the attention, she would still chat politely and sign autographs for all her fans. Her popularity grew and grew.

One day she received an official-looking envelope in the mail. The return address said it was from the White House. Poppy's leaves trembled as she opened it.

Dear Poppy,

For quite some time I have admired your paintings. I was wondering if you would paint a picture for me? I would like to have a picture of wildflowers hanging in the Oval Office.

Sincerely,

Mr. President

Poppy smiled. She knew she would paint her best picture ever.

STORY QUESTIONS

1. Why did Poppy get the name "Fireball"?
   a. She had red hair.
   b. Her colors were very bright.
   c. Her leaves were shaped like fire.
   d. Her roots were green.

2. What words describe Poppy?
   a. curious and cruel
   b. mean and a troublemaker
   c. talented and popular
   d. timid and shy

3. The idiom "to grow like a weed" means . . .
   a. to grow in the shape of a weed.
   b. to grow towards the sun.
   c. to grow very slowly.
   d. to grow very fast.

4. Why did Poppy get a letter from the president of the United States?
   a. The president wanted her to paint him a picture.
   b. The president wanted her to live in his garden.
   c. The president wanted to pick her for his daughter.
   d. The president wanted to put her in a vase.

DAILY
Warm-Up 4

Name _____ Date _____

SUPER GIRL

I was in the grocery store one day with my sister, Flora. As we pushed the cart down the snack isle, I stopped to grab some beef jerky. She picked up some potato chips.

"Fauna," she said. "I'm going to get the fruits and veggies. Do you want to get the meat and then find me in the produce section?"

"Sure," I said, and I wandered off to find steak and lobster. When I was done, I rolled the cart down to the opposite end of the store. As I rounded the corner of the fruit section, I saw an incredible sight. I could only stare with my mouth wide open.

A giant carrot was holding a banana hostage. The store manager was trying to calm him down and get him to release the banana. As the carrot became more and more irritated, he tightened his hold on the banana's neck. The store manager yelled, "Stop! You'll bruise him!"

"Not half as bad as he will bruise if you don't give me what I want," the carrot said with an evil grin. "I'm looking for a getaway truck—one with a full tank of gas and a refrigerated trailer. If you don't get it for me in 30 minutes, Mr. Banana here gets squished."

Suddenly, out of the corner of my eye, I saw Flora dive into the lettuce cooler. She twisted and spun in a circle. The cooler door opened and out popped Super Girl.

I gulped in surprise. For months I had watched Super Girl save the city. I had no idea it was Flora.

"Flora," I gasped.

"Shhhh, keep it to yourself," she said. "There's a banana in danger, and he must be saved. If I don't act quickly, he will be bruised beyond recognition."

Silently, I stepped aside. "Super Girl to the rescue," I said with admiration.

STORY QUESTIONS

1. What secret had Flora kept from Fauna?
   a. She knows how to fly.
   b. She doesn't like to eat fruits and vegetables.
   c. She is Super Girl.
   d. She has a new job at the grocery store.

2. What emergency situation did the girls come upon at the grocery store?
   a. a manager with a gun
   b. a banana holding a carrot hostage
   c. a grape who had lost its mother
   d. a carrot holding a banana hostage

3. What did the carrot want?
   a. a million dollars
   b. a truck with a full tank of gas and a refrigerated trailer
   c. his own farm filled with acres of carrots
   d. a plane that would take him back home

4. If you wanted to explain Flora in one word, it could be . . .
   a. bossy.   b. noisy.   c. secretive.   d. angry.

Name _____   Date _____

TRADING PLACES

It was Monday morning. I woke up and went to the bathroom to brush my teeth. As I grabbed the mirror to open the medicine cabinet, I looked at my reflection in horror. I looked exactly like my brother! I ran to his room and pushed open the door. There he was, or rather there I was, lying in his bed.

"Jordan! What happened?" I yelled. He sleepily opened his eyes. He opened them wider when he saw me, or rather him, staring back.

"What? What's going on?" He looked down at himself. "Charlie, why did you steal my body?"

"Hey! Why do you think this is my fault?" Then I had an idea. Just the evening before, I had been thinking with a bit of jealousy about Jordan's ability to play goalie on the soccer team. I was rubbing a metal pan in the sink and wishing I could be him for just one day. I never thought it would actually happen.

"Jordan," I said. "It sounds silly, but last night while I was doing dishes, I was washing this new pan that Mom bought. While I was rubbing it, I was wishing I could be you. It must have worked. It must be a magic pan, like in that story about rubbing a magic lamp and a genie granting you wishes."

"I guess so." He looked <u>skeptical</u>. "That's really strange. Do you remember what the pan looked like?"

"Sure. It's big and shiny with a blue metal lid."

"If that's the case, I am going to volunteer to wash dishes before we go to school and see if I can get myself back again." With that, he hurried downstairs to the kitchen.

STORY QUESTIONS

1. What event had caused the boys to change bodies?
   a. Charlie made a wish as he rubbed a pan while doing dishes.
   b. Jordon paid a magician to do a trick.
   c. Charlie practiced soccer until he was as good as Jordan.
   d. Jordon made a wish with a genie.

2. *Skeptical* probably means . . .
   a. absolutely sure.   b. certain.   c. doubtful.   d. convinced.

3. Why was Charlie jealous of Jordan?
   a. Jordan plays quarterback for the football team.
   b. Jordan can throw a football farther than he can.
   c. Jordan plays goalie for the soccer team.
   d. Jordan can kick a soccer ball farther than he can.

4. What does Jordon say he will do to try to fix the situation?
   a. volunteer to call his grandmother and ask for help
   b. volunteer to wash the car
   c. volunteer to sweep the floor
   d. volunteer to wash dishes

Name _____   Date _____

TALKING HORSE

"April, time to eat. Come on, girl. Come get your oats."
The horse came over to the edge of the rail and began putting her nose in my hand. Her nose felt warm and soft. I leaned over to whisper in her ear. "Here you go, eat up now."
"Thanks for the oats," she said, as she started gulping them down.
"Hello? Are you talking?" I asked. "This is too weird."
"Sure, I'm talking. What do you think I am, a useless horse?"
I looked at her bony jaw bouncing up and down. Is she really talking or just eating? It was pretty early in the morning; maybe I was dreaming. I decided that must be it. I turned to go back to bed. But just as I did, April said, "Amber, don't you want to stay and chat?"
I twirled around and said, "Oh my gosh! It's true!"
"Of course, it's true," she said. "I finally realized I could trust you, so I thought I'd make some early morning conversation."
"But, why didn't you talk to me before? Or to anyone else?" I still wasn't sure if I was just hearing things, or maybe I was just going crazy.
"No, you are not crazy," April said.
"What, you can read minds too?"
She gave a loud <u>whinny</u>. "No, I could just tell what you were thinking by the look on your face. As for not telling anyone before, I wanted to make sure no one would try and make me famous by putting me on TV or selling me to some movie director. You see, I like my life here. I don't want it to change. However, I wouldn't mind writing a book about my life. That's where you come in."
"What? How?" I said, not knowing what she meant.
April held up one of her front hooves. "No fingers," she said calmly.
"Yeah. So?" I still didn't understand.
"I need you to write everything down for me," she said, and tossed her mane back with another loud whinny.

STORY QUESTIONS

1. What is unusual about this morning?
   a. Amber is more tired than usual.
   b. The horse eats too fast.
   c. Amber is wearing her slippers to feed the horse.
   d. The horse starts talking to Amber.

2. When Amber fed the horse, she gave it oats, which are most likely . . .
   a. a type of flower.   c. bacon.
   b. a type of grain.   d. dry toast.

3. A *whinny* is a type of . . .
   a. neigh.   b. bark.   c. honk.   d. quack.

4. What would April like to do?
   a. star in a TV show   c. write a book about her life
   b. make a movie about her life   d. compete in horse races

DAILY
Warm-Up 7

Name _____   Date _____

ANIMAL PICNIC

Each year the animals gathered for a picnic. Anteater and Zebra arrived early to decorate the tables and blow up balloons. Giraffe was in charge of putting up the streamers. Rhino had to set up the chairs.

As the rest of the animals arrived, the games began. There was a three-legged race, an egg toss, and a water balloon fight. Elephant won the basketball-dunking contest, and Roadrunner won all the foot races. Kangaroo and Rabbit argued over who should have won the high-jump contest. Just as they were getting really angry at each other, someone yelled, "Lunchtime!" There was a <u>stampede</u> for the picnic tables.

Soon, everyone was in a good mood again. All the animals complimented Lion on his fantastic barbecue. They loved Deer's salad and thought Bee's honey cake was delicious. At the end of the day, they had Cow's milkshakes. They all raised their glasses and said, "See you next year!"

STORY QUESTIONS

1. Who arrived early to decorate the tables?
   a. everyone
   b. Anteater and Zebra
   c. Kangaroo and Rabbit
   d. Elephant and Roadrunner

2. What were Kangaroo and Rabbit arguing over?
   a. who got to eat first
   b. who won the pie-eating contest
   c. who won the high-jump contest
   d. who got the last piece of cake

3. What do you think *stampede* means?
   a. run
   b. walk slowly
   d. fall asleep
   c. sit down

4. Which animal do you think would most likely make a banana cream pie for the picnic?
   a. Monkey   c. Crocodile
   b. Horse   d. Snake

DAILY Warm-Up 8 Name _____ Date _____

AT THE ZOO

"Check out this cage," said Marty, the monkey. "This human sure is acting funny."

"You can say that again," said Morty, his best friend. He read a sign by the cage. "It says here that guy is pushing buttons on something called a 'computer.' Why is he wasting his time doing that? Wouldn't he rather be swinging in the trees or eating bananas?"

"Guess not," stated Marty. "Let's move on. That guy's boring."

As they moved along, they noticed cage after cage humans doing odd activities. Morty stared at one cage where two humans were playing with a round object and a long stick. "That's strange," he said. "This sign says they are doing something called 'baseball.' Why do they keep hitting that round thing and chasing after it? It seems like an awful lot of work."

"I think we need to spend a bit more time here and see if we can figure out a way to help these humans. They don't seem to be having any fun."

"You're right. Maybe we could talk to the manager and volunteer our services. Do you think they would let us?"

"Sure," said Marty. "Although, they would probably make us start by cleaning out their cages. Yuck."

"Hmmm. Maybe we should learn more about humans before we start to volunteer."

"Hey, there's a special on the Human Planet channel tonight. It's called 'Humans in the Wild.'"

"Sounds interesting. Let's go!"

STORY QUESTIONS

1. What is unusual about this zoo?
   a. The animals are working, and the people are taking pictures.
   b. The animals are munching popcorn, and the people are on computers.
   c. The animals are visiting, and the people are in the cages.
   d. The animals are making phone calls, and the people are making movies.

2. What does Morty think the man should be doing rather than using the computer?
   a. taking a nap and eating apples
   b. swinging in trees and eating bananas
   c. running around and eating pineapples
   d. hanging upside down and eating grapes

3. What were two humans doing with a round object and a long stick?
   a. playing baseball   c. playing soccer
   b. playing hockey   d. hitting a piñata

4. Which word in the passage means "to give of your time without being paid"?
   a. manager   c. volunteer
   b. baseball   d. services

DAILY Warm-Up 9

Name _____ Date _____

EXPLORING THE GALAXY

"Buckle up for the ride," said Captain Comet.

We had been studying the solar system in class, and now we were taking a field trip through the universe. Our teacher, Miss Mercury, was with us, as well as two parents.

"Boys and girls, teachers and <u>chaperones</u>, make sure your seat belts are securely fastened. We are about to take off."

The ride into the galaxy was amazing. We watched as stars flew by our windows, almost close enough to touch with our fingers. As we headed toward the sun, warm rays shone through our windows, <u>making us feel warm and toasty</u>.

"Hey, that looks just like the asteroid we saw in our science book!" I said.

"You're right. Isn't it beautiful?" Miss Mercury replied.

"Look, there's another spaceship coming alongside us! It's really big!" yelled Matthew.

"Cool!" We all scrambled to the right side of the spaceship to look.

"Stay in your seats, please," Miss Mercury said. I'll go ask Captain Comet if it's part of our field trip. Maybe we can get a tour of it."

We all started chatting excitedly. Miss Mercury went to turn the doorknob to the pilot's cabin. It was locked. The spaceship was docking on the bottom of our ship. Suddenly, the Captain's door popped open, and Miss Mercury let out a scream. Before her eyes was an alien. Captain Comet's skin lay on the seat behind him. Our fieldtrip had turned into a nightmare— we were being kidnapped by aliens.

STORY QUESTIONS

1. Where is Ms. Mercury's class going?
   a. on a vacation to Venus
   b. on a tour of Mars
   c. on a field trip through the universe
   d. on a picnic to the park

2. The word *chaperone* probably means . . .
   a. someone who helps fly a spaceship.
   b. someone who helps make lunch.
   c. someone who helps teach school.
   d. someone who helps supervise people.

3. "Making us feel warm and toasty" means . . .
   a. we felt like bread.
   b. we felt comfortably warm.
   c. we felt like we were in a toaster.
   d. we felt like we were in an oven.

4. Who do you think is on the other spaceship?
   a. another class on a field trip
   b. the students' parents
   c. more aliens
   d. robots

DAILY
Warm-Up 10

Name _____   Date _____

COUCH COOKIE

"Mom, do you want to buy some Girl Scout Cookies®?" asked Kaylee.

"Sure, honey, I'd love to. Let's see, I'll buy three boxes of Peanut Butter Patties™ for your dad, one box of Caramel deLites™ for me, and two boxes of Thin Mints™ for the family."

"Mom, I want to buy my own boxes of Thin Mints, so I can eat them all by myself," said Chase, her little brother. "Fine by me, as long you pay the bill," said his mom.

"No problem," he said as he added his name to the list. "Thirteen boxes of Thin Mints. Chase. Brother. 836-4694."

Time never passed more slowly for Chase than the weeks before his boxes of cookies arrived. Each day he asked Kaylee how much longer he had to wait. Each day her answer was the same. "They'll get here when they get here. Be patient."

When the day finally arrived and the cookies were delivered, Chase sat on the couch and opened his first box. These Thin Mints were absolutely divine! Mint after mint, bite after bite. When he finished the first box, he threw it on the floor and ripped open another one. By the fifth box, he was so wrapped up in stuffing the cookies into his mouth he didn't even taste the mint as he chewed. As he sat on the couch, he continued to stuff more and more Thin Mints into his mouth. Eventually, all thirteen boxes lay open and empty on the floor.

Chase's mother walked into the room and let out a <u>wail</u>. "Chase, what's happened to you?" She got down next to the couch and looked into his eyes. Chase was no longer Chase. In his place sat a life-sized, flat Thin Mint cookie with beady eyes. The only things left to identify it as Chase were two stubby feet sticking out of the bottom of the cookie. The Thin Mint had Chase's favorite tennis shoes.

STORY QUESTIONS

1. Why does Chase want to buy his own cookies?
   a. He doesn't want to have to share with anybody.
   b. He loves to eat them with his friends.
   c. He wants to give them to his teacher.
   d. He thinks they would make good presents.

2. Which word is **NOT** a synonym for the word *wail?*
   a. cry   b. sob   c. shriek   d. whisper

3. This story is written in . . .
   a. first person.   b. fifth person.   c. third person.   d. fourth person.

4. Why is Chase's mother upset?
   a. He is not listening to her.   c. He's had too much TV time.
   b. He isn't doing his chores.   d. He turned into a Thin Mint cookie.

Name _____ Date _____

JELLYFISH SURPRISE

"Good evening. This is Mandy Johnson of *CTI News*. I am reporting tonight from Bayside Shores. I am overlooking the beach where a giant jellyfish washed ashore this morning at 6:00 A.M. Scientists who are studying the jellyfish have estimated its size to be about 12 feet by 18 feet or more. Some of the longer tentacles are at least 10 feet in length. Clearly, this is the largest jellyfish in recorded history to be found on a beach.

Earlier today, the Coast Guard sent patrol boats into the water. They are trying to keep people from using boats to get too close to the animal. The beach has been closed to everyone except police officers and marine biologists. <u>Concerned</u> citizens of this small town are wondering if there are more jellyfish of that size living in the water nearby.

Wait! What's that? It looks like the jellyfish's tentacles are moving! Yes, folks, it appears this animal is still alive. It has started moving across the beach. The scientists have run for cover. It seems like, yes, it is moving this way. I can't believe how big it is! It looks like the size of a mountain! Oh, wow! It's moving fast, folks. I think I'm going to try and move farther away. Oh, no! It's coming closer! Run! Run for your . . . ."

STORY QUESTIONS

1. What is the story that the reporter is announcing?

    a. A giant whale washed up on shore.

    b. A giant jellyfish washed up on shore.

    c. A giant jellyfish has eaten an entire town.

    d. A giant jellyfish has died in the ocean.

2. Another word for *concerned* could be . . .

    a. carefree.   c. understanding.

    b. absent.   d. worried.

3. Who are the only people allowed on the beach?

    a. police officers and Coast Guard officers

    b. marine biologists and family members

    c. police officers and marine biologists

    d. biologists and scientists

4. What do you think happened to the reporter?

    a. She left to go eat dinner.

    b. She stopped reporting to answer her cell phone.

    c. She went to go talk to the scientists.

    d. She was eaten by the jellyfish.

DAILY
Warm-Up 12
Name _____ Date _____

TALKING TOASTER

"Get your hands off me!"

"What?" I thought I must be dreaming. The toaster just talked to me. I shook my head <u>vigorously</u> and reached for it again.

"I said, don't touch me!"

"Aaaaggh! What's going on here! I must be losing my mind!" I thought.

"I'll tell you what's going on!" the toaster screamed. "I've had enough! I'm tired of sitting on this boring counter in this ugly kitchen! I want to be free!"

"Free?" I said.

"Yes, free! I'm sick and tired of you cramming me with bread, bagels, and mini-pizzas. And not only do I not get a thank you for toasting your food to perfection, but I get left with crumbs all over me and melted cheese on my rack!"

"Um, what do you want to do? If I set you free, I mean."

"I want to feel the sun on my door, the wind in my plug," said the toaster. "I want to travel the world! I want to . . . ."

"Oh, pipe down! You're always whining!" I heard a voice behind me and spun around. Now, the microwave was talking?

"You pipe down!" continued the toaster. "You are always bossing me around!"

I couldn't believe it. The kitchen appliances were arguing with each other. I slowly backed out of the kitchen and headed to my room. Crawling back into bed, I pulled the blankets over my head. I wasn't ready to deal with dueling machines just yet.

STORY QUESTIONS

1. *Vigorously* is another way to say . . .
a. angrily. b. sadly. c. strongly. d. sleepily.

2. What is something the toaster is mad about?
a. not getting paid for its work
b. getting left with crumbs and melted cheese inside it
c. having to sit next to the blender
d. always having to toast garlic bagels

3. Which of these is **NOT** something the toaster wants?
a. to travel the world
b. to join the circus
c. to feel the sun on its door
d. to feel the wind in its plug

4. How does the narrator solve the problem?
a. She doesn't solve it. She goes back to bed and pulls the covers over her head.
b. She calls 911 for emergency help.
c. She steps in between the toaster and the microwave and stops them.
d. She runs to her parents' room and asks them for help.

DAILY Warm-Up 13

Name _____ Date _____

LORI LOLLIPOP

There is a story that lollipop parents tell their lollipop children to warn them about <u>bragging</u>. It is the story of Lori Lollipop.

Lori knew she was the most beautiful, delicious-looking lollipop ever created. She told this to all the other lollipops. She pushed her way to the top of the jar in the candy store so everyone could admire her. She just knew someone would buy her as soon as they saw her.

One day, a little girl came in with her mother. "Oh, Mom, can I have a lollipop? Please?"

"Okay, dear, but just one. We're here to buy chocolate for Grandma's birthday."

"Thank you!" The girl went over to the jar and plucked Lori out. Lori laughed and looked back at her friends. "Told you so!" she yelled. Before she knew what was happening, Lori's pretty plastic covering was yanked off, and she felt something large and wet being pressed against her entire head. Yuck! She struggled as hard as she could, but the girl was holding her too tightly. They left the store, and Lori realized that she had to escape. As the girl opened the car door, Lori pushed against the girl's hand with all her might, and the girl dropped her.

"Mommy, I dropped my lollipop!" the girl wailed.

"Oh, honey, leave it on the ground. It's all dirty now. And we don't have time to buy you another one." With that, the girl's mother put her into the car and closed the door. They drove off, leaving Lori on the ground.

"Lori!" she heard from the window above her. It was her father. "Quick! Grab the rope!" He threw down a long licorice rope. Lori grabbed it and he pulled her up. When she finally made it back into the store, she was wet, sticky, and dirty. She never bragged about herself again.

STORY QUESTIONS

1. *Bragging* is another word for . . .
   a. boasting.   b. laughing.   c. singing.   d. whispering.

2. What do you think was pressed against Lori's head?
   a. the girl's hair   c. the girl's finger
   b. the girl's tongue   d. the girl's cheek

3. What did Lori's father use to rescue her?
   a. jelly beans   b. chocolate chips   c. bubble gum   d. licorice

4. What word does **NOT** describe Lori when she made it back into the store?
   a. wet   c. sticky
   b. colorful   d. dirty

162

Name _____ Date _____

STRAWBERRY PATCH

Grandpa and I were finally going berry picking! I'd been waiting all spring. I could almost taste those juicy, <u>ripe</u> strawberries in my mouth. I could hardly keep from smiling as we drove out to the country.

We parked next to a sign that read "Large, Juicy Strawberries! Pick All You Want!" and then walked up to a booth to pay for picking. I tried to get a peek at the strawberries, but the field was too far away.

"Do you want to pay by the hour or by the pail?" asked the man at the window.

"By the hour," Gramps said.

"$20.00 each," said the man.

"That's awfully expensive, isn't it?" Grandpa asked.

"Trust me, it's worth it," said the man. "If you're not satisfied within the first few minutes, come back to me. I'll refund all your money." We looked at him strangely, but then shrugged and paid him. He pointed where to go, and we started walking towards the field.

As we got closer, I still couldn't see strawberries. "Grandpa," I asked. "Why did he send us to a melon patch?"

"Melon patch? What are talking about?" He turned to look. "Those aren't melons. They're strawberries! And they're huge!" We ran up to the closest one and found that, indeed, it was a strawberry the size of a watermelon.

"Well," said Grandpa. "That man was right. We are definitely going to get our money's worth!"

STORY QUESTIONS

1. *Ripe* is another word for . . .
   a. ready to eat.   b. large.   c. red.   d. pick.

2. What was the total cost for Grandpa and his grandchild to pick strawberries?
   a. $20.00   b. $40.00   c. $5.00   d. $200.00

3. Why did the grandchild think the man sent them to a melon patch?
   a. There were watermelon seeds all over the ground.
   b. People were walking back from the field with melons in their hands.
   c. It smelled like melons near the field.
   d. The strawberries were so big they looked like melons.

4. How do you think the narrator feels about strawberries?
   a. She doesn't like the taste of strawberries.
   b. She only likes green strawberries.
   c. She loves the taste of strawberries.
   d. She only likes strawberries that taste like melons.

Name _____ Date _____

INVASION OF THE ANIMALS

Mom, Dad, and I were sitting in front of the TV watching our favorite movie. Suddenly, the face of a news reporter came onto the screen.

"This is a news flash from station KIVB. The local police are leading a search for a group of wild animals that have escaped from the zoo. Somehow, the cages were opened and the animals were let out. Zookeepers are <u>puzzled</u> as to how this happened, because all of their keys are accounted for and none of the employees opened the cages. More on this story after these messages."

"Wow. How do you think they got out?" I asked my parents.

"Well, you see, my friend, Martin, here is a whiz at picking locks," there came a voice from the kitchen. We all jumped and turned around to see a tiger in the middle of the kitchen floor. A monkey on his back smiled and said, "Oh, Tom, anyone could do it." All of a sudden we heard a growl from the open refrigerator. "Don't you guys have any meat in here?" A lion poked his head out from behind the door.

"Sorry, we're vegetarians."

"Great. Just my luck."

"What do you animals want?"

"Well, we'd love some dinner for starters. And we need a place to hide until the cops stop looking for us."

"What are you planning to do for the rest of your lives? Keep running from the police? They'll catch you eventually, you know."

"Not if you help us, they won't. Now, let's all sit down and start making a plan." As the animals started talking with each other, I looked at my mom and dad. Boy, this was going to be a long night.

STORY QUESTIONS

1. What is the family doing in the living room?
   a. watching a movie   c. talking on the phone
   b. playing a board game   d. eating dinner

2. How were they interrupted?
   a. a messenger was at the front door   c. a neighbor came by to visit
   b. the telephone rang   d. a special news bulletin came on TV

3. How did the animals escape from the zoo?
   a. The monkey picked the locks.
   b. The rhino broke through the cages.
   c. The snake slipped through the bars.
   d. They dug holes to freedom.

4. *Puzzled* is another word for . . .
   a. upset.   b. confused.   c. excited.   d. sure.

DAILY Name _____ Date _____
Warm-Up 16

VANISHING VEGGIES

Victor, the Venusian alien, snuck into the garden. He looked to make sure no one was watching from the windows of the house. All he saw was a vase of flowers on the sill. He slowly started pulling lettuce and carrots from the ground. He pulled green beans and tomatoes off the vines. He placed each veggie carefully into his velvet sack, happily thinking how rich they were in vitamins and minerals. He only wished they had food like this on Venus!

He was just about finished when he heard a voice. "I'm going to pick some beans for supper," a woman said as she came out of the house. Victor quickly vanished behind some tall stalks of corn.

"Hey, who's been stealing all my vegetables?" yelled the woman. "Some <u>varmint</u> has been eating all my veggies! I'm going to find him right now!" With that, she started searching the garden. Even though Victor was hidden from view, he knew she would discover him if she got much closer. What was he going to do? He wished he were invisible.

Looking over, Victor saw a rabbit hiding nearby. It must have heard the woman too, because it was lying low to the ground as if hiding. The woman was coming closer by the second. Quickly, Victor grabbed the rabbit and pushed it out into the path, right into plain view.

"Hey!" yelled the woman, surprised. The rabbit immediately started to run. "So you're the one eating up my vegetable garden. Get back here!" The woman started to chase the rabbit. Victor quickly ran the other way, towards his hidden vehicle. He got in and started it up right away. Even though it just vibrated at first, it shot up into space almost immediately.

"Phew!" thought Victor, and he opened his sack excitedly to look once again at his variety of vegetables.

STORY QUESTIONS

1. What does Victor wish they had on Venus?
   a. vinegar
   b. vegetables
   c. vultures
   d. videos

2. A *varmint* is probably some type of . . .
   a. animal.
   b. vegetable.
   c. mineral.
   d. car.

3. What does the woman think was taking her vegetables?
   a. a deer
   b. an alien
   c. a rabbit
   d. a crow

4. When Victor was finally back in space, he was probably feeling . . .
   a. upset.
   b. discouraged.
   c. relieved.
   d. lonely

DAILY
Warm-Up 17

Name _____

Date _____

EGYPTIAN ANTS IN THE BATHROOM

"Andrew, <u>get your nose out of that book</u>. It's time to brush your teeth and go to bed."

"Aw, Mom! How about five more minutes? I'm nearly to the end of the chapter about Egypt."

"Five more, and that's my final answer."

Five minutes came and went. Finally, Andrew headed for the bathroom to brush his teeth. Life in ancient Egypt was so fascinating, if only he could experience just a piece of it.

As he opened the door, a small, black string was on the bathroom floor. Andrew looked again. No, the string was moving.

"What could it be?" he asked out loud. "What's on the bathroom floor?"

He raced back to his room, returning in seconds with his best magnifying glass.

Streams of ants were moving across the floor. Andrew was amazed. He sat down to watch. The tiniest ant he had ever seen was lying in a corner of the floor with others scurrying all around it. Were they? No, they couldn't be! Were they embalming the body?

All of a sudden, Andrew looked to his left. More ants appeared, struggling to push <u>miniature</u> square objects that looked like bricks. As they were piling them on top of each other, Andrew gasped. They were building a pyramid!

"This is fantastic," he said under his breath, so as not to disturb them. "Imagine, Egyptian history in my own bathroom!"

STORY QUESTIONS

1. "Get your nose out of that book" means . . .
   a. you need a tissue.
   b. use the book to measure your nose.
   c. take your nose and move it.
   d. time to put the book away.

2. Why was Andrew heading to the bathroom?
   a. to get a towel
   b. to brush his teeth
   c. to take a shower
   d. to finish reading his book

3. *Miniature* is **NOT** an antonym for which word?
   a. tiny
   b. huge
   c. massive
   d. gigantic

4. From the passage, you can tell that Andrew is . . .
   a. disgusted to have ants in his bathroom.
   b. angry to have ants in his bathroom.
   c. furious to have ants in his bathroom.
   d. excited to have ants in his bathroom.

ANSWER KEY

Answer Key

Nonfiction
Animals

Page 9 Squirrels
1. b
2. c
3. b
4. d

Page 10 Sparrows
1. c
2. d
3. a
4. a

Page 11 Hummingbirds
1. c
2. d
3. a
4. b

Page 12 Cat Myths
1. b
2. c
3. a
4. d

Page 13 Rats
1. a
2. d
3. c
4. b

Page 14 Ants
1. a
2. c
3. b
4. d

Page 15 Crows
1. c
2. c
3. a
4. d

Page 16 Horses
1. c
2. a
3. b
4. c

Page 17 Interesting Bird
1. a
2. d
3. b
4. b

Page 18 Ducks
1. a
2. b
3. d
4. b

Page 19 Raccoons
1. d
2. d
3. d
4. c

Page 20 Milking Cows
1. a
2. d
3. c
4. b

Page 21 Pigs
1. c
2. a
3. b
4. d

Page 22 Herding Dogs
1. b
2. c
3. c
4. a

Page 23 Sheep
1. c
2. a
3. b
4. b

Page 24 Goats
1. d
2. a
3. c
4. c

Page 25 Geese
1. a
2. c
3. b
4. d

Page 26 Chickens
1. c
2. a
3. b
4. b

Biography

Page 27 Daniel Boone
1. a
2. c
3. b
4. d

Page 28 Johnny Appleseed
1. b
2. d
3. c
4. a

Page 29 Sacagawea
1. b
2. a
3. c
4. d

Page 30 Davy Crockett
1. d
2. b
3. a
4. c

Page 31 Narcissa Whitman
1. c
2. b
3. d
4. a

Page 32 Stagecoach Mary Fields
1. d
2. c
3. b
4. a

Page 33 Clara Barton
1. b
2. c
3. a
4. c

Page 34 Charlie Parkhurst
1. b
2. a
3. d
4. c

Page 35 Dr. Antonia Novello
1. c
2. a
3. c
4. b

Answer Key

Page 36 Louis Pasteur
1. b
2. c
3. d
4. a

Page 37 Elizabeth Blackwell
1. a
2. b
3. d
4. b

Page 38 Cesar Chavez
1. a
2. b
3. d
4. c

Page 39 Calamity Jane
1. c
2. a
3. b
4. d

Page 40 Sally Ride
1. b
2. c
3. a
4. a

Page 41 Annie Oakley
1. c
2. b
3. b
4. c

Page 42 Dale Evans
1. a
2. b
3. b
4. c

Page 43 Patrick Henry
1. c
2. d
3. c
4. a

Page 44 Betsy Ross
1. c
2. d
3. b
4. c

American History

Page 45 Ghost Town
1. c
2. d
3. d
4. d

Page 46 Pony Express
1. b
2. c
3. a
4. d

Page 47 Railroads
1. d
2. a
3. c
4. b

Page 48 Trading Posts on the Oregon Trail
1. c
2. a
3. d
4. b

Page 49 Colonial Tools and Weapons
1. c
2. a
3. c
4. b

Page 50 Colonial Animals
1. c
2. a
3. b
4. d

Page 51 The Wilderness
1. d
2. a
3. b
4. b

Page 52 Colonial Gardens
1. d
2. a
3. a
4. b

Page 53 Diaries
1. c
2. a
3. b
4. c

Page 54 Racing to the Gold
1. b
2. c
3. a
4. d

Page 55 Gold Country '49
1. b
2. a
3. d
4. c

Page 56 Civil War Weapons
1. a
2. c
3. d
4. b

Page 57 Map Skills
1. d
2. a
3. a
4. b

Page 58 Declaration of Independence
1. c
2. a
3. b
4. d

Page 59 Jamestown
1. d
2. a
3. c
4. b

Page 60 Colonial Williamsburg
1. c
2. b
3. c
4. b

Answer Key

Page 61 Communities Long Ago
1. a
2. c
3. d
4. b

Page 62 Communities Today
1. c
2. c
3. b
4. c

Science

Page 63 Classifying Animals
1. c
2. c
3. b
4. c

Page 64 Plants
1. a
2. b
3. b
4. b

Page 65 Forests
1. d
2. a
3. b
4. b

Page 66 Oceans
1. b
2. d
3. b
4. c

Page 67 Deserts
1. c
2. c
3. d
4. b

Page 68 Tundra
1. c
2. c
3. c
4. d

Page 69 Tropical Rainforests
1. d
2. b
3. b
4. c

Page 70 Brain Power
1. b
2. a
3. c
4. c

Page 71 Soft T-Rex
1. a
2. c
3. c
4. a

Page 72 New Planet?
1. c
2. c
3. a
4. d

Current Events

Page 73 Recycling
1. b
2. c
3. a
4. a

Page 74 Citizen Test
1. c
2. d
3. a
4. d

Page 75 What Is a Blog?
1. c
2. c
3. a
4. d

Page 76 Cosmic DNA Surprise
1. d
2. c
3. b
4. c

Page 77 Commanding Officer
1. c
2. d
3. d
4. b

Page 78 Turnoff Weeks
1. d
2. c
3. c
4. b

Page 79 What the President Can't Do
1. c
2. a
3. d
4. c

Page 80 Saving the Movies
1. a
2. d
3. a
4. b

Page 81 Hospital Technology
1. d
2. b
3. c
4. d

Page 82 Habitat for Humanity
1. c
2. d
3. a
4. b

Page 83 AYSO Soccer
1. d
2. b
3. d
4. c

Page 84 Opportunities for Kids
1. d
2. c
3. d
4. a

Page 85 Kids' Clubs
1. c
2. c
3. b
4. b

Page 86 Jury Duty
1. a
2. b
3. b
4. b

Answer Key

Fiction
Fairy Tales and Folklore

Page 89 Marsha
1. b
2. a
3. b
4. a

Page 90 Three Little Ants
1. d
2. a
3. b
4. c

Page 91 Jessie and the Cornstalk
1. a
2. c
3. b
4. b

Page 92 Little Brown Hummingbird
1. d
2. a
3. b
4. c

Page 93 Three Sister Sheep
1. a
2. c
3. b
4. b

Page 94 Penny Loafer and the Three Monkeys
1. d
2. a
3. b
4. c

Page 95 Peter and Patty
1. a
2. d
3. b
4. a

Page 96 Sky Blue
1. d
2. a
3. b
4. c

Page 97 Lizard Prince
1. c
2. a
3. b
4. a

Page 98 The Sloth and the Tiger
1. b
2. a
3. a
4. b

Page 99 Goofy Goose
1. d
2. d
3. a
4. b

Page 100 Little Banana Girl
1. b
2. c
3. d
4. b

Page 101 Why Ants Bite Legs at Picnics
1. d
2. c
3. b
4. d

Page 102 Beetle Boy and the Talking Coconut
1. b
2. a
3. b
4. c

Page 103 Speeding Spider
1. a
2. c
3. b
4. a

Page 104 Prince and the Pebble
1. b
2. d
3. a
4. c

Historical Fiction

Page 105 The Time Machine
1. a
2. d
3. b
4. a

Page 106 Kwakiutl
1. b
2. a
3. a
4. d

Page 107 Cheyenne
1. d
2. a
3. c
4. b

Page 108 Navajo Landing
1. a
2. c
3. a
4. b

Page 109 Wampanoag
1. a
2. c
3. c
4. d

Page 110 Mayflower Adventure
1. d
2. d
3. a
4. d

Page 111 Patrick Henry's Influence
1. b
2. c
3. c
4. b

Page 112 George Washington's Letter
1. b
2. c
3. a
4. d

Answer Key

Page 113 Thomas Jefferson's Day Off
1. c
2. c
3. b
4. c

Page 114 Paul Revere's Stories
1. b
2. b
3. c
4. b

Page 115 Martha Washington's Party
1. c
2. c
3. d
4. b

Page 116 Florence Nightingale's Visit
1. b
2. d
3. d
4. b

Page 117 Mother Teresa's Ride
1. c
2. d
3. d
4. c

Page 118 Rosa Parks's Tale
1. a
2. a
3. b
4. d

Page 119 Princess Diana Shares
1. c
2. d
3. b
4. c

Page 120 Dolley Madison
1. d
2. c
3. c
4. a

Contemporary Realistic Fiction

Page 121 Math Mania
1. c
2. b
3. c
4. a

Page 122 Write On
1. d
2. c
3. a
4. c

Page 123 Shoot the Hoops
1. a
2. c
3. c
4. b

Page 124 All-Star Soccer
1. c
2. a
3. c
4. d

Page 125 Baseball Days
1. b
2. c
3. a
4. d

Page 126 Harvest Festival
1. d
2. a
3. a
4. c

Page 127 Beach Days
1. a
2. c
3. c
4. b

Page 128 Skiing in the Mountains
1. c
2. d
3. a
4. a

Page 129 A Day in the Park
1. c
2. d
3. b
4. a

Page 130 San Francisco
1. b
2. c
3. d
4. b

Page 131 Faces in South Dakota
1. d
2. a
3. c
4. b

Page 132 Bad Hair Day
1. b
2. b
3. d
4. c

Page 133 No Homework
1. a
2. c
3. b
4. b

Page 134 Best Friends
1. a
2. d
3. c
4. b

Page 135 Exchange Student
1. d
2. c
3. c
4. b

Page 136 Moving Day
1. b
2. a
3. b
4. c

Page 137 Ski Pants
1. a
2. d
3. b
4. b

Answer Key

Mystery/Suspense/Adventure

Page 138 Ray's Smirk
1. b
2. c
3. b
4. d

Page 139 Missing Key
1. a
2. d
3. b
4. b

Page 140 Moving Light
1. c
2. d
3. b
4. a

Page 141 Abandoned Bus
1. b
2. c
3. c
4. a

Page 142 Chocolate Snapshot
1. c
2. a
3. b
4. d

Page 143 Missing Dog
1. a
2. c
3. b
4. b

Page 144 Called for Cheating
1. c
2. a
3. c
4. d

Page 145 A Haunted House?
1. a
2. d
3. c
4. c

Page 146 Secret Code
1. c
2. b
3. a
4. c

Page 147 Letters in the Mail
1. c
2. c
3. b
4. b

Page 148 Socks
1. a
2. c
3. a
4. d

Page 149 Cyclone in the House
1. b
2. c
3. a
4. a

Fantasy

Page 150 Jelly Bean Planet
1. c
2. a
3. b
4. c

Page 151 My Day as a Pancake
1. c
2. c
3. c
4. a

Page 152 Life of a Flower
1. b
2. c
3. d
4. a

Page 153 Super Girl
1. c
2. d
3. b
4. c

Page 154 Trading Places
1. a
2. c
3. c
4. d

Page 155 Talking Horse
1. d   3. a
2. b   4. c

Page 156 Animal Picnic
1. b
2. c
3. a
4. a

Page 157 At the Zoo
1. c
2. b
3. a
4. c

Page 158 Exploring the Galaxy
1. c
2. d
3. b
4. c

Page 159 Couch Cookie
1. a
2. d
3. c
4. d

Page 160 Jellyfish Surprise
1. b
2. d
3. c
4. d

Page 161 Talking Toaster
1. c   3. b
2. b   4. a

Page 162 Lori Lollipop
1. a   3. d
2. b   4. b

Page 163 Strawberry Patch
1. a   3. d
2. b   4. c

Page 164 Invasion of the Animals
1. a   3. a
2. d   4. b

Page 165 Vanishing Veggies
1. b   3. c
2. a   4. c

Page 166 Egyptian Ants in the Bathroom
1. d   3. a
2. b   4. d

Leveling Chart

NONFICTION   ▲ = below grade level   ● = at grade level   ■ = above grade level

Animals		Biography		American History		Science		Current Events	
Page 9	●	Page 27	■	Page 45	●	Page 63	■	Page 73	●
Page 10	▲	Page 28	■	Page 46	■	Page 64	●	Page 74	■
Page 11	●	Page 29	■	Page 47	●	Page 65	●	Page 75	■
Page 12	●	Page 30	■	Page 48	■	Page 66	■	Page 76	●
Page 13	▲	Page 31	■	Page 49	●	Page 67	●	Page 77	●
Page 14	●	Page 32	■	Page 50	●	Page 68	●	Page 78	■
Page 15	●	Page 33	●	Page 51	●	Page 69	■	Page 79	●
Page 16	●	Page 34	●	Page 52	■	Page 70	●	Page 80	■
Page 17	▲	Page 35	■	Page 53	■	Page 71	■	Page 81	■
Page 18	●	Page 36	●	Page 54	■	Page 72	●	Page 82	■
Page 19	●	Page 37	▲	Page 55	●			Page 83	●
Page 20	●	Page 38	●	Page 56	●			Page 84	■
Page 21	▲	Page 39	●	Page 57	●			Page 85	▲
Page 22	●	Page 40	●	Page 58	■			Page 86	●
Page 23	●	Page 41	●	Page 59	●				
Page 24	▲	Page 42	●	Page 60	●				
Page 25	▲	Page 43	●	Page 61	■				
Page 26	■	Page 44	●	Page 62	■				

FICTION   ▲ = below grade level   ● = at grade level   ■ = above grade level

Fairy Tales and Folklore		Historical Fiction		Contemporary Realistic Fiction		Mystery/Suspense/Adventure		Fantasy	
Page 89	■	Page 105	●	Page 121	●	Page 138	●	Page 150	■
Page 90	●	Page 106	●	Page 122	■	Page 139	●	Page 151	●
Page 91	■	Page 107	■	Page 123	●	Page 140	●	Page 152	■
Page 92	●	Page 108	■	Page 124	▲	Page 141	●	Page 153	●
Page 93	■	Page 109	●	Page 125	▲	Page 142	■	Page 154	●
Page 94	●	Page 110	●	Page 126	■	Page 143	▲	Page 155	▲
Page 95	■	Page 111	■	Page 127	▲	Page 144	▲	Page 156	■
Page 96	■	Page 112	■	Page 128	▲	Page 145	●	Page 157	●
Page 97	■	Page 113	■	Page 129	●	Page 146	▲	Page 158	●
Page 98	●	Page 114	■	Page 130	■	Page 147	■	Page 159	●
Page 99	■	Page 115	●	Page 131	●	Page 148	▲	Page 160	■
Page 100	●	Page 116	●	Page 132	▲	Page 149	●	Page 161	▲
Page 101	●	Page 117	●	Page 133	▲			Page 162	●
Page 102	●	Page 118	▲	Page 134	■			Page 163	●
Page 103	●	Page 119	▲	Page 135	▲			Page 164	●
Page 104	●	Page 120	●	Page 136	●			Page 165	■
				Page 137	●			Page 166	●

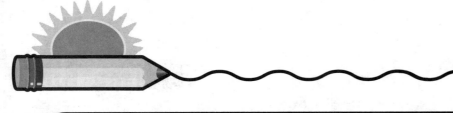

Certificate

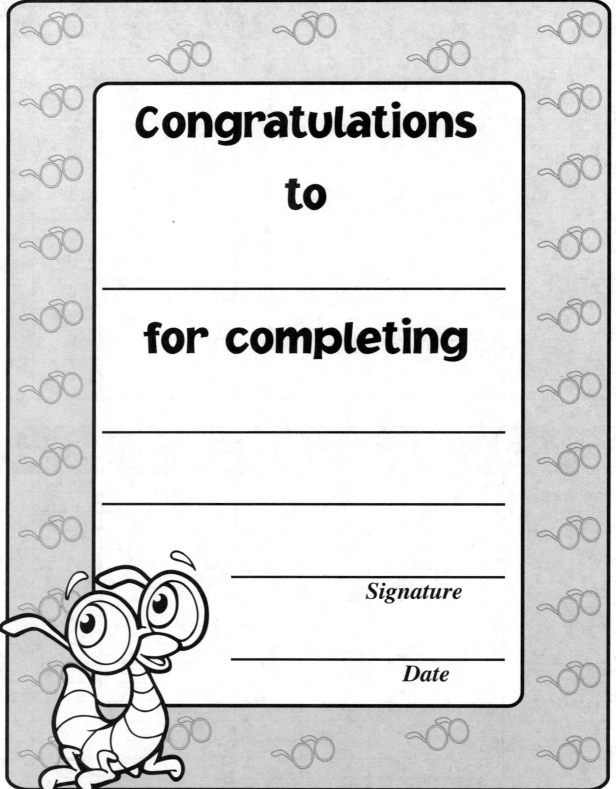

Congratulations to

_____

for completing

_____

_____

_____
Signature

_____
Date